P9-EEI-513

California
Preschool
Learning
Foundations

Volume 3

History–Social Science
Science

Publishing Information

The *California Preschool Learning Foundations (Volume 3)* was developed by the Child Development Division, California Department of Education. This publication was edited by Faye Ong, working in cooperation with Laura Bridges, Consultant, Child Development Division. It was designed and prepared for printing by the staff of CDE Press, with the cover and interior design created by Cheryl McDonald. It was published by the Department of Education, 1430 N Street, Sacramento, CA 95814-5901. It was distributed under the provisions of the Library Distribution Act and *Government Code* Section 11096.

© 2012 by the California Department of Education
All rights reserved

ISBN 978-8011-1727-5

Ordering Information

Copies of this publication are available for sale from the California Department of Education. For prices and ordering information, please visit the Department Web site at http://www.cde.ca.gov/re/pn or call the CDE Press Sales Office at 1-800-995-4099.

Notice

The guidance in the *California Preschool Learning Foundations (Volume 3)* is not binding on local educational agencies or other entities. Except for the statutes, regulations, and court decisions that are referenced herein, the documents is exemplary, and compliance with it is not mandatory. (See *Education Code* Section 33308.5.)

Contents

A Message from the State Superintendent of Public Instruction

I am delighted to present the *California Preschool Learning Foundations (Volume 3)*. This publication is part of a three-volume series designed to improve early learning and development for California's preschool children.

Young children are naturally eager to learn. We encounter their amazing curiosity at every turn. Their wonder about the world extends to understanding of human traditions and activity. They also ask about how the physical world works. However, even with their great curiosity about the world of people and things, not all young children enter kindergarten ready for school. All too often, some already lag behind their classmates, which may adversely affect their continued learning and development in kindergarten and beyond. High-quality preschool teaching connects with young children's strong interest in concepts and processes from the history–social science and science domains while contributing to long-range social and academic success.

Children who attend high-quality preschools benefit from rich opportunities to learn through play. Their play focuses on the world around them—for example, social roles rooted in human history and culture and the life of their community. They also playfully experiment with living and nonliving things and discover how they change. Children thrive when offered a curriculum that integrates all domains in a way that is culturally and linguistically meaningful and appropriate to their development.

With the goal of ensuring that all pre-schools in California offer high-quality programs, the California Department of Education collaborated with leading early childhood educators, researchers, advocates, and parents to develop Volume 3 of the preschool learning foundations.

The foundations outline key knowledge and skills that most children can acquire when provided with the kinds of interactions, instruction, and environments shown by research to promote early learning and development. Volume 3 focuses on two domains: history–social science and science. These domains have received less attention than some other domains, but their importance has been increasingly recognized by early childhood education experts.

As research that is summarized in this volume indicates, young children are naturally drawn to concepts and processes in history–social science and science. They look to their families and their teachers to help them explore these learning domains. High-quality teaching builds on children's interests and engages them in making sense of social and physical phenomena.

Efforts to provide children with high-quality preschool experiences fit into the overall mission of both the Department and the federal Head Start program. Learning and development that occurs before a child enters preschool is as important as the learning and development that occurs during the school years. A continuum of learning and development begins early in life and continues through higher education. Understanding the links between the different ages and different early childhood services allows educators to see how to build on children's earlier learning and prepare children for the next educational challenge. To foster greater understanding of children's learning and development during the first five years, this volume explains the connections among the infant/toddler learning and development foundations, preschool learning foundations, Common Core State Standards, kindergarten content standards, and the *Head Start Child Development and Early Education Framework.* An investment in high-quality care and education programs throughout the early years will promote learning for all children and ensure school readiness when they enter kindergarten.

These foundations will help guide and support all California preschools in providing developmentally appropriate instruction and activities that engage young hearts and minds. Such learning will lead to children's well-being and success throughout life.

Tom Torlakson

TOM TORLAKSON
State Superintendent of Public Instruction

Acknowledgments

The development of the preschool learning foundations involved many groups: project leaders; lead researchers; the expanded research consortium; the preschool learning foundations research consortium; staff from the California Department of Education; early childhood education stakeholder organizations; facilitators of the draft review sessions and the participants; and participants in the Web posting process.

Project Leaders

The following staff members are gratefully acknowledged for their contributions: **Peter Mangione** and **Charlotte Tilson**, WestEd.

Lead Researchers

Special thanks are extended to the lead researchers for their expertise and contributions as lead writers. Note: The names, titles, and affiliations of the individuals listed in these acknowledgments were correct at the time the publication was developed.

History–Social Science

Janet Thompson, University of California, Davis

Ross Thompson, University of California, Davis

Science

Osnat Zur, WestEd

Expanded Research Consortium

Volume 3 was developed by an expanded research consortium. Domain experts and their affiliations are identified below. These individuals contributed their expertise to this project and collaborated with the preschool learning foundations research consortium.

History–Social Science

Oscar Barbarin, Tulane University

Barbara Bowman, the Erikson Institute and the Chicago Public Schools

Amy Obegi, Solano Community College

Carolyn Pope Edwards, University of Nebraska, Lincoln

Michael Lopez, National Center for Latino Child and Family Research

Gayle Mindes, DePaul University

Science

Marco Bravo, San Francisco State University and Santa Clara University

Caroline Carney, Monterey Peninsula College

Lucia French, University of Rochester

Rochel Gelman, Rutgers University

Karen Lind, Illinois State University

Art Sussman, WestEd

Sandra Waxman, Northwestern University

Preschool Learning Foundations Research Consortium

The following research consortium members are recognized for their knowledge and expertise in guiding the development process and for their expert review of volume 3 to reflect California's young learners.

Melinda Brookshire, WestEd
Peter Mangione, WestEd
Katie Monahan, WestEd
Caroline Pietrangelo Owens, WestEd
Teresa Ragsdale, WestEd
Amy Schustz-Alvarez, WestEd
Charlotte Tilson, WestEd
Ann-Marie Wiese, WestEd
Osnat Zur, WestEd

English–Language Development and Cultural Diversity Advisers

Vera Gutierrez-Clellen, San Diego State University

Gisela Jia, The City University of New York and Lehman College

Antonia Lopez, National Council of La Raza

Alison Wishard Guerra, University of California, San Diego

Universal Design Advisers

Maurine Ballard-Rosa, California State University, Sacramento

Linda Brault, WestEd

California Department of Education (CDE)

Thanks are also extended to the following CDE staff members: **Geno Flores**, Chief Deputy Superintendent; **Cindy Cunningham**, Deputy Superintendent, P–16 Policy and Information Branch; **Camille Maben**, Director, Child Development Division; **Cecelia Fisher-Dahms**, Administrator, Quality Improvement Office; and **Desiree Soto**, Administrator, and **Laura Bridges**, Consultant, Child Development Division, for ongoing revisions and recommendations. During the lengthy development process, many CDE staff members were involved at various levels. Additional thanks are extended to **Gail Brodie**, **Sy Dang Nguyen**, **Luis Rios**, **Mary Smithberger**, and **Charles Vail**, Child Development Division; **Meredith Cathcart**; Special Education Division; and to **Gavin Payne**, **Michael Jett**, **Gwen Stephens**, **Anthony Monreal**, and **Rick Miller**.

Early Childhood Education Stakeholder Organizations

Representatives from many statewide organizations provided perspectives affecting various aspects of the learning foundations.

Action Alliance for Children
Alliance for a Better Community
Asian & Pacific Islanders California Action Network (APIsCAN)
Association of California School Administrators
Baccalaureate Pathways in Early Childhood Education (BPECE)
Black Child Development Institute (BCDI), Sacramento Affiliate
Child Care and Development Fund, Administration for Children and Families Region IX Federal/State/Tribes Collaboration Workgroup
California Alliance of African American Educators (CAAAE)
California Association for Bilingual Education (CABE)
California Association for the Education of Young Children (CAEYC)
California Association of Family Child Care (CAFCC)
California Association of Latino Superintendents and Administrators (CALSA)
California Child Care Coordinators Association
California Child Care Resource and Referral Network (CCCRRN)
California Child Development Administrators Association (CCDAA)
California Child Development Corps
California Commission on Teacher Credentialing
California Community College Early Childhood Educators (CCCECE)
California Community Colleges Chancellor's Office (CCCCO)
California County Superintendents Educational Services Association (CCSESA)
California Early Reading First Network
California Federation of Teachers (CFT)
California Head Start Association (CHSA)
California Kindergarten Association
California Preschool Instructional Network (CPIN)
California Professors of Early Childhood Special Education (CAPECSE)
California School Boards Association
California State Parent Teacher Association

Note: The names and affiliations of the individuals were current at the time the document was developed.

California State University Office of the Chancellor
California Teachers Association
Californians Together
Campaign for High Quality Early Learning Standards in California
Child Development Policy Institute
Children Now
The Children's Collabrium
Coalition of Family Literacy in California
Council for Exceptional Children/The California Division for Early Childhood (Cal DEC)
Council of CSU Campus Childcare (CCSUCC)
Curriculum Alignment Project
Curriculum and Instruction Steering Committee
English Language Learners Preschool Coalition (ELLPC)
Fight Crime, Invest in Kids California
First 5 Association of California
First 5 California (California Children and Families Commission)
Head Start State-Based Training and Technical Assistance Office for California
Infant Development Association of California (IDA)
Learning Disabilities Association of California
Los Angeles Universal Preschool (LAUP)
Mexican American Legal Defense and Education Fund (MALDEF)
Migrant Education Even Start (MEES)
Migrant Head Start
National Council of La Raza (NCLR)
Packard Foundation Children, Families, and Communities Program
Preschool California
Professional Association for Childhood Education (PACE)
Special Education Administrators of Country Offices (SEACO) Committee
Special Education Local Plan Area (SELPA) Committee
TeenNOW California
University of California Child Care Directors
University of California Office of the President (UCOP)
Voices for African American Students, Inc. (VAAS)
ZERO TO THREE

Draft Review Sessions

Special thanks are also extended to **Nancy Herota, Natalie Woods Andrews** of the California Preschool Instructional Network, and **Melinda Brookshire, Jenna Bilmes,** and **Jan Davis** of WestEd, for their contributions in facilitating 54 review sessions on the draft foundations. Thanks also go to the participants in the draft review sessions for their contributions to this project.

Introduction

The preschool learning foundations are critical to the California Department of Education's (CDE's) efforts to strengthen preschool education and close the school-readiness gap in California. The foundations describe competencies—knowledge and skills—that most children can be expected to exhibit in a high-quality program as they complete their first or second year of preschool. In other words, the foundations identify paths of learning that, with appropriate support, children typically move along during the preschool years.

The foundations are designed to promote understanding of young children's development of knowledge and skills and to help teachers, program administrators, families, and policymakers consider appropriate ways to support children's learning. In essence, the foundations serve as a cornerstone for informing early childhood educators about children's learning and development. The foundations are to be used in combination with other sources of information. These sources include formal educational course work on early learning and development; information on individual differences (especially disabilities); knowledge about the contribution of cultural and linguistic experiences to early development and English-language development, including the CDE's resource guide *Preschool English Learners: Principles and Practices to Promote Language, Literacy, and Learning* (2007); insights from children's families; and the practical experiences of preschool teachers and program directors.

The support that young children need to attain the competencies varies from child to child. Many children learn simply by participating in high-quality preschool programs. Such programs offer children environments and experiences that encourage active, playful exploration and experimentation. With play as an integral part of the curriculum, high-quality programs include purposeful teaching to help children gain knowledge and skills. As for the history–social science and science foundations, children can demonstrate their knowledge and skills by using any language and, for most of the foundations, nonverbal forms of expression. Many children effectively apply their advanced ability in their home language to understand concepts from the history–social science and science domains. Other children may have a disability or special need that requires particular adaptations.* To serve all children, preschool programs must provide appropriate social interactions, experiences, and environments and sensitively assist each child's learning and development.

All 50 states either have developed preschool standards or are in the process of doing so. Many states have aligned early learning standards with kindergarten

---

*Adaptations should be coordinated with the child's family and any specialist working with the child.

content standards. In most cases, these alignment efforts focused on academic content areas such as English–language arts or mathematics. In California, priority has been placed on aligning expectations for preschool learning with the Common Core State Standards for English–language arts and literacy in history/social studies, science, and technical subjects and for mathematics, and with the state's academic content standards for kindergarten. Equally important, those content areas are complemented by attention to social–emotional development and English-language development. Like the learning in domains such as language and literacy and mathematics, the concepts in social–emotional development and English-language development also contribute significantly to young children's readiness for school (Shonkoff and Phillips 2000; Bowman, Donovan, and Burns 2000; NAEYC 2002). Because the focus on preschool learning in California includes the full range of developmental domains, the term *foundations* is used rather than *standards.* This term is intended to convey that learning and development in every domain is integrated with all other domains and affects young children's readiness for school.

Content of This Volume

The preschool learning foundations presented in this volume cover the following domains:

- History–social science
- Science

The domains above represent crucial areas of learning and development for young children. The foundations written for each of the domains are based on research evidence and are enhanced with expert practitioners' suggestions and examples. The foundations in a particular domain provide a thorough overview of development in that domain. Preschool children's knowledge and skills can be considered from the perspective of one domain, such as history–social science or science. Yet when taking an in-depth look at a specific domain, one needs to keep in mind that learning is an integrated experience for young children. For example, at any given moment, a young child may concentrate on a single science concept, but the experience may also pertain to learning in the cognitive, social, linguistic, physical, and health domains. The relationships between learning domains are particularly apparent between the history–social science and social–emotional development domains and between the science and mathematics domains. Close inspection of the foundations shows that all of the preschool learning domains intersect with one another and that closely related foundations occasionally appear in two or more domains.

Overview of the Foundations

The strands for each of the domains discussed previously are listed in this section.

History–Social Science Domain

The history–social science foundations address an area that is receiving increasing attention in preschool curricula. These foundations focus on the following five strands:

1. *Self and Society,* which centers on culture and diversity, relationships, and social roles and occupations
2. *Becoming a Preschool Community Member (Civics),* which pertains to skills for democratic participation, responsible conduct, fairness and respect for other people, and conflict resolution
3. *Sense of Time (History),* which includes understanding past events, anticipating and planning future events, personal history, and historical changes in people and the world
4. *Sense of Place (Geography and Ecology),* which covers navigating

familiar locations, caring for the natural world, and understanding the physical world through drawings and maps

5. *Marketplace (Economics)*, which focuses on the economic concept of exchange

The foundations for this domain reflect the many ways in which young children learn about basic concepts of history–social science. Young children explore concepts related to history–social science that are rooted in the cultural experiences of their families and communities. The history–social science foundations, which center on young children's capacity to operate as members of a community, complement the social–emotional development foundations, which describe how young children express and regulate their emotions and develop social understanding and skills.

Science Domain

The science domain consists of the following four strands:

1. *Scientific Inquiry*, which pertains to observation and investigation and to documentation and communication
2. *Physical Sciences*, which focuses on the properties and characteristics of nonliving objects and materials and the changes in nonliving objects and materials
3. *Life Sciences*, which addresses properties and characteristics of living things and changes in living things
4. *Earth Sciences*, which covers properties and characteristics of earth materials and objects and changes in the earth

The competencies covered by the science domain center on content that connects with the natural curiosity of preschool children. Early in life, children rely on cultural experiences in their homes and communities to engage in inquiry and understand the properties and characteristics of nonliving and living objects and materials, and earth materials and objects. The scientific concepts and methods addressed by the preschool curriculum give children added perspective as they build their knowledge and skills in the science domain.

Organization of the Foundations

Each strand consists of substrands, and the foundations are organized under the substrands. Foundations are presented for children at around 48 months of age and at around 60 months of age. In some cases, the difference between the foundations for 48 months and 60 months is more pronounced than for the other foundations. Even so, the foundations focus on 48 and 60 months of age because they correspond to the end of the first and second years of preschool. In all cases, the foundation at around 60 months of age builds on the corresponding foundation at around 48 months of age. In other words, for each foundation the age levels are two points on a continuum of learning. Of course, teachers need to know where each child is on a continuum of learning throughout the child's time in preschool.

The preschool Desired Results Developmental Profile (DRDP–PS), which has been aligned with the preschool foundations, volume 1, and will be aligned with the foundations in volumes 2 and 3, gives teachers a means to observe children's learning along a continuum. On the continuum, children at the earliest level of development start to become familiar with a new knowledge area and, in a basic way, try out skills they are starting to learn. At the next level, children begin to demonstrate basic mastery in a knowledge and skill area. That level is followed by one in which children refine and expand their knowledge and skills in an area of learning; at the latest developmental level on the continuum, they connect the knowledge and skills they have mastered in one area with those in other areas. The Desired Results Developmental Profile *access* provides a means to observe the knowledge and skills of preschool children with disabilities whose development is best described within a birth-to-age-five range.

The examples listed under each foundation suggest possible ways in which children may demonstrate the competency addressed by a foundation. The examples illustrate different kinds of contexts in which children may show the competencies reflected in the foundations. Examples highlight that children learn while engaging in imaginative play, exploring the environment and materials, making discoveries, being inventive, or interacting with peers, teachers, or other adults. Many examples include children using language to express themselves. Of particular note, children can demonstrate learning in these domains in any language and often do so nonverbally. For instance, children who are English learners will often understand history–social science and science through their home language and culturally meaningful experiences at home and in their community and express such knowledge in their home language. Although the examples often illustrate the diversity of young children's learning experiences, they are not exhaustive. In fact, teachers often observe other ways in which young children demonstrate the competency addressed by a foundation.

In addition, one needs to be cautious about how the examples are used. They are intended to illustrate possible behaviors rather than to function as assessment items or to present curricular strategies. Using the examples to compare individual children to a group or to measure individual children's progress would be inappropriate. Young children demonstrate their knowledge and skills in various ways. Some may act in ways that reflect the examples. Others may demonstrate their competencies through behaviors that are quite different from the examples and

in many different languages. To use the examples effectively, one must be mindful of the context of the early learning setting, community, and the culture or cultures of each group of preschool children.

Note: Appendix A, "The Foundations," contains a summary list of the foundations in each domain, without examples.

Universal Design for Learning

The California preschool learning foundations are guides to support preschool programs in their efforts to foster the learning and development of all young children in California, including children who have disabilities. It is important for the preschool foundations to provide opportunities to follow different pathways to learning, so that the foundations will be helpful for all of California's children. To that end, the foundations incorporate a concept known as *universal design for learning.*

The Center for Applied Special Technology (CAST) developed the principles for universal design for learning based on the understanding that children learn in different ways (CAST 2007). In today's diverse preschool settings and programs, the use of a curriculum accessible to all learners is critical to successful early learning. Universal design for learning is not a single approach that will accommodate everyone; rather, it provides multiple approaches to learning in order to meet the needs of diverse learners. Universal design provides for *multiple means of representation, multiple means of engagement,* and *multiple means of expression* (CAST 2007). *Multiple means of representation* refers to providing information in a variety of ways so the learning needs of all children are met. *Multiple means of engagement* refers to providing choices of activities in the setting or program that facilitate learning by building on children's interests. *Multiple means of expression* refers to allowing children to use alternative methods to demonstrate what they know or what they feel.

The examples given in the preschool learning foundations have been worded to incorporate multiple means of receiving and expressing. This has been accomplished by the variety of examples for each foundation and the use of inclusive language, as follows:

- When consistent with the content being illustrated, the terms *communicates* and *responds* are used in examples rather than *says*. "Communicates" and "responds" are inclusive of any language and any form of communication, including speaking, sign language, pictures, electronic communication devices, eye-pointing, gesturing, and so forth.
- The terms *identifies, indicates,* and *points to* are used to represent multiple means of indicating objects, people, or events in the environment. Examples include the use of gestures, eye-pointing, nodding, or responding *yes* or *no* when another person points to or touches an object.

When reading each foundation and the accompanying examples, teachers can consider the means by which a child with a disability might best acquire information and demonstrate competence in those areas. It is essential to include a child's special education teacher, parents, or related service provider when planning environments, curriculum, and adaptations. In addressing the individual needs of children, early childhood educators need to consider the enormous variation in children's growth and development across all developmental domains.

For example, when consulting with a special education teacher, family members, or related-service provider, one may learn that a child with physical disabilities and visual impairments can understand many concepts without being able to demonstrate them in the same way as other children. Although the child may show delays in one area of development, it does not necessarily indicate delays in other areas

of development such as cognitive development. This distinction is important to keep in mind because if an early childhood educator expects a child who cannot see or physically move to demonstrate a level of understanding, the child's cognitive abilities may be underestimated as he or she may be limited in the ability to consistently and broadly show the expected level. Even so, without the appropriate specialized instruction, materials, and adaptations, a child may show cognitive delays. The preschool years are a time of critical cognitive growth and concept development, and one cannot assume that this development will simply occur in children with disabilities when a sensory or motor disability is present. It is essential that teachers collaborate with family members and special educators to ensure that all children with disabilities are provided with effective preschool experiences and appropriate educational services and supports.

Alignment of the Preschool Learning Foundations with Other Key Resources

The *California's Preschool Learning Foundations, Volumes 1–3,* are designed to align with content standards in key early childhood resources. A comprehensive analysis of the alignment of the *California Preschool Learning Foundations* with the *California Infant/Toddler Learning and Development Foundations,* the California content standards for kindergarten, the *Common Core State Standards* (CCSS) for kindergarten, and the *Head Start Child Development and Early Learning Framework (Head Start Learning Framework)* may be viewed at http://www.cde.ca.gov/sp/cd/re/documents/reversealignment.pdf. Appendix B presents an overview of this alignment. It identifies the connections between foundations/standards drawn from different resources and illustrates the developmental progression along a continuum, from birth to kindergarten, in different developmental domains (e.g.,

Language and Literacy, Mathematics; Physical Development). For example, the overview summarizes the alignment across the infant/toddler learning and development foundations in language and literacy, the preschool learning foundations in language and literacy and the kindergarten CCSS in English language arts. The overview of the alignment also details the links between the *California Preschool Learning Foundations* and the *Head Start Learning Framework*. These key resources share the common purpose of supporting young children's learning and development, and the alignment document highlights their shared goals and content.

The Foundations and Preschool Learning in California

The foundations are at the heart of the CDE's approach to promoting preschool learning. Teachers use best practices, curricular strategies, and instructional techniques that assist children in learning the knowledge and skills described in the preschool learning foundations. The "how-tos" of teaching young children include setting up environments, supporting children's self-initiated play, selecting appropriate materials, and planning and implementing teacher-guided learning activities. Two major considerations underlie the "how-tos" of teaching. First, teachers can effectively foster early learning by thoughtfully considering the preschool learning foundations in the planning of environments and activities. And second, during every step in planning for young children's learning, teachers have an opportunity to tap into the prominent role of play. Teachers can best support young children both by encouraging the rich learning that occurs in children's self-initiated play and by introducing purposeful instructional activities that playfully engage preschoolers in learning.

Professional development is a key component of fostering preschool learning. The foundations can become a unifying element for both preservice and in-service professional development. Preschool program directors and teachers are encouraged to use the foundations to facilitate curriculum planning and implementation. The foundations are designed to help teachers intentionally focus their efforts on the knowledge and skills that all young children need for success in preschool and early elementary school and throughout life.

References

Bowman, B. T., M. S. Donovan, and M.S. Burns, eds. 2000. *Eager to Learn: Educating Our Preschoolers.* Washington, DC: National Academies Press.

California Department of Education. 2007. *Preschool English Learners: Principles and Practices to Promote Language, Literacy, and Learning.* 2nd ed. Sacramento: California Department of Education.

Center for Applied Special Technology (CAST). 2007. Universal Design for Learning. http://www.cast.org/udl/ (accessed June 8, 2007).

NAEYC (National Association for the Education of Young Children). 2002. *Early Learning Standards: Creating the Conditions for Success.* Washington, DC: NAEYC.

Scott-Little, C., S. L. Kagan, and V. S. Firelow. 2006. "Conceptualization of Readiness and the Content of Early Learning Standards: The Intersection of Policy and Research." *Early Childhood Research Quarterly* 21: 153–73.

Shonkoff, J. P., and D. A. Phillips, eds. 2000. *From Neurons to Neighborhoods: The Science of Early Childhood Development.* National Research Council and Institute of Medicine, Committee on Integrating the Science of Early Childhood Development. Washington, DC: National Academies Press.

FOUNDATIONS IN
History–Social Science

This section describes foundations for development in history–social science by preschoolers. The goal of the California Department of Education (CDE) in developing these foundations is to describe the knowledge and skills that are typical of preschool children who make progress toward readiness for kindergarten. Volume 3 describes, based on developmental research, behavior reflecting age-appropriate competencies in relevant areas of history and social science for children at around 48 and 60 months of age.

The development of preschool foundations for history–social science is based on the assumption that competencies in a wide variety of areas prepare children for school. Education prepares children for a broad range of adult responsibilities and goals; therefore children's appreciation for history, culture, geography, economics, civics and citizenship, the global environment, and individual identity in a cultural and racial context is essential to their education, as are basic capacities in language, mathematics, and the physical sciences. An early start in preschool helps children learn about themselves in a social and human context, enabling them to acquire a deep understanding of the responsibilities of members of a democratic society, their place in a complex economy, the legacy of past generations who contributed to society, and an appreciation of the richness and diversity of other people.

Scope of the Foundations

Social science is a branch of learning that pertains to how people live together in the social world. Young children are beginning to think about the social world and their place in it. They are interested in the similarities and differences between people and in how people interact with the natural world (such as animals and plants). They are also interested in how social rules help people to get along and the roles and responsibilities that they and other people assume. Children are developing a sense of time—how their current experience is affected by their personal past and relates to their future. They are developing a sense of belonging to places and locations that are meaningful to them. They are also developing a basic understanding of how the economic world operates and their role in it. The foundations focus on these aspects of their developing understanding.

The preschool foundations for history–social science were created in relation to the *History–Social Science Content Standards for California Public Schools, Kindergarten Through Grade Twelve* (CDE 2005). The content standards for kindergarten through grade twelve emphasize both the development of children's age-appropriate knowledge of history and social science and the growth of analytical and reasoning skills to promote their own inquiry in those domains. The foundations were also prepared with attention to the 10 themes in social studies identified by the National Council for the Social Studies (NCSS): (1) culture; (2) time, continuity, and change; (3) people, places, and environments; (4) individual development and identity; (5) individuals, groups, and institutions; (6) power, authority, and governance; (7) production, distribution, and consumption; (8) science, technology, and society; (9) global connections; and (10) civic ideals and practices (http://www.socialstudies. org/standards/strands) (accessed November 16, 2011). The foundations are organized according to strands and substrands that generally align with those of the NCSS but do not follow the exact NCSS terminology and order. For example, although it will be many years before preschoolers are ready to study geography, the early years are when young children acquire a "sense of place" manifested in their familiarity with locations and larger terrains where they live and play, a growing interest in the natural world and caring for it, and their experimentation with drawings and mapmaking.

Although young children have lim-ited historical understanding, they do have a "sense of time." It is shown by their talk about events of the recent past, a sense of their own development over time, an autobiographical memory, and anticipation of future events and planning for them. Young children are also active in the marketplace and exhibit a dawning understanding of the world of goods and money that will contribute, many years later, to the study of economics.

Young children also learn about responsibility and the processes of democracy through their participation in an early childhood education program. In preschool, many gain their first experience in the responsibilities of group membership: they make decisions after discussion, vote, respect majority opinion, participate in the creation and enforcement of classroom rules, learn how to treat others fairly and respectfully, cooperate with others, and develop skills in managing conflict with peers and adults.

More broadly, preschoolers are also beginning to understand how they fit within broader social systems beyond the family. They are interested in and rehearse adult roles and occupations, learn about the mutual obligations of relationships, and encounter cultural, ethnic, and racial diversity by which they learn about themselves and others. What young children learn in an early childhood education setting builds, of course, on what they learn at home about the responsibilities of family members, the importance of treating others fairly and respectfully, and family identity and culture (Perez-Granados and Callanan 1997). Because civic participation, culture, conflict resolution, and mutual respect remain important throughout life, the

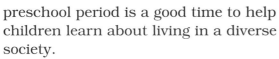
preschool period is a good time to help children learn about living in a diverse society.

During the preschool years, children grow in their understanding of the social world in which they live. The social world includes several areas of knowledge:

- Self and Society (beginning to identify with how their family does things and understand that other families and people have ways of doing things that are different or similar to what their family does)
- Civics (how to live with others and how rules work, such as taking turns to go down the slide)
- History (events that happened in the past, even before they were born, such as when their mommy was a little girl)
- Geography (the location of familiar places in relation to each other, such as knowing the way to preschool or that the park is across the street from the grocery store) and the different kinds of places where people live
- Ecology (learning to take care of earth and animals [for example, not wasting water])
- Economics (a beginning understanding of money and the exchange of things and services, such as groceries purchased at the store)

The foundations were developed to help teachers focus on supporting young children's growing understanding in these areas of knowledge.

The foundations of history–social science consist of the following strands and substrands:

Self and Society

1.0 Culture and Diversity
2.0 Relationships
3.0 Social Roles and Occupations

Becoming a Preschool Community Member (Civics)

1.0 Skills for Democratic Participation
2.0 Responsible Conduct
3.0 Fairness and Respect for Other People
4.0 Conflict Resolution

Sense of Time (History)

1.0 Understanding Past Events
2.0 Anticipating and Planning Future Events
3.0 Personal History
4.0 Historical Changes in People and the World

Sense of Place (Geography and Ecology)

1.0 Navigating Familiar Locations
2.0 Caring for the Natural World
3.0 Understanding the Physical World Through Drawings and Maps

Marketplace (Economics)

1.0 Exchange

These strands and substrands are less familiar in the field of early childhood education than those for domains such as social–emotional development. Recent work at the national level by the NCSS and preschool standards of various states reflect a growing interest in topics such as becoming a preschool community member, sense of time, and sense of place. Although perhaps new for some early childhood educators, this terminology makes visible the learning that often occurs in the preschool setting. With an increased awareness of the history–social science domain, early childhood educators have an opportunity to be intentional in supporting learning in this domain and integrating history–

social science learning with learning in other domains.

The foundations in history–social science share some similarities with other foundations, particularly those in social–emotional development. The resemblance is expected. As learning is integrated across different domains of understanding, children's achievements in different areas naturally overlap. The development of responsible conduct, social relationships, and conflict-resolution skills, which are core features of healthy social–emotional growth, are also essential components of learning to become a constructive member of a community. Although these social-science foundations emphasize the child in the context of the group more than do the social–emotional foundations, teachers should be aware that similar developmental achievements are relevant to each domain. In addition, the history–social science foundations build on the foundations in English-language development, especially the following challenges: displaying competencies in a language that is different from the home and claiming community membership for children who are culturally diverse.

Purpose of the Foundations

For each substrand, behavioral descriptions of age-appropriate competencies are provide, together with examples of the behaviors. Bibliographic notes for each substrand provide an expanded description of the developmental accomplishments relevant to the topic, citations to the research literature, further information for teachers and administrators, and some suggestions for relevant program practices. The CDE will also create a curriculum framework in history–social science to provide preschool teachers with specific practices to foster developing competencies in these areas. References and source materials are included at the end of this chapter.

To use this information appropriately, it is important to remember two things. First, the examples for each foundation are meant to be guidelines for understanding children's learning and development, not assessment items or a curriculum framework. The examples clarify these competencies by providing concrete illustrations of specific behaviors. They are not intended to be yardsticks to measure the behavior of certain children in a teacher's group, nor should they be turned into assessment tools. The reason for this precaution is that preschoolers may demonstrate their competencies in a variety of ways. Some may do so consistently in the same way as the examples provided; others may demonstrate their skills using alternative behaviors and in many different languages. Children are different from one another, and their behavior may differ from the examples but still be appropriate for their age. The examples accompanying each foundation should be used in consideration of the context of the child's early learning environment, community, and culture. Second, the Bibliographic Notes included in this chapter are meant to be a teaching tool for administrators, supervisors, instructors, and teachers so they can learn more about the development of the children in their care. The notes refer to useful research about young children.

Educators, early childhood specialists, developmental scientists, and others involved in efforts to describe the behaviors typical of children at around 48 months compared with children at around 60 months will find themselves humbled by the realization that the developmental changes apparent over the course of a single year may be subtle. Sometimes individual differences in the characteristics and behavior of children at any age may be greater than the average behavioral changes they will experience over the course of a year of development in various areas.

The purpose of these foundations, therefore, is to highlight the developmental differences that are most common between typical children at around 48 and 60 months of age. The differences between children of each age may be subtle, but some consistent themes run throughout these foundations. Although children at 48 and 60 months of age do not have a sophisticated sense of time, place, or the marketplace, older children demonstrate a more complex and nuanced understanding of each. Older children are more capable of seeing themselves in a context of time and location and take greater initiative in learning more. Compared with younger children, children at around 60 months of age also have an enhanced psychological awareness of themselves and others and a greater capacity for self-control that permits greater skill in social responsibility, conflict management, and citizenship.

Finally, older children in this age range are more capable of social relationships that are mutual and reciprocal in quality, which contributes to greater skill in group participation and responsibility. In general, these developmental differences should be apparent across the different foundations described in this chapter.

Understanding the Foundations

The foundations were written with the assumption that *young children have access to appropriate social interactions, experiences, and environments that normally support healthy development.* Young children who grow up in settings that lack opportunities for learning, healthy self-expression, and positive interactions with others cannot be expected to show the kinds of developmental achievements of children who live in more supportive settings. Children in a typical early education setting will vary along the continuum of support and positive learning opportunities available to them outside the preschool. Sensitive teachers must provide early learning experiences that are well suited to each child.

In addition, these foundations were written to describe typical development rather than to describe aspirations for optimal growth. On occasion, the behavior of young children is described in ways that reflect undesirable but entirely age-appropriate characteristics. For example, young children experience conflict with other children and clash even more with their friends than they do with other children (Hartup 1996; Rubin, Bukowski, and Parker 2006; Rubin and others 2005). Young children often are self-interested in their negotiations with other people and do not act as generously or sympathetically as adults would desire (Dunn 1993; Shonkoff and Phillips 2000; Thompson 1998).

Research shows that young children tend to prefer the culture, ethnicity, race, and practices of their families and may act critically toward children or adults who are different from them (Aboud 1988, 2003, 2008; Barbarin and Odom 2009; Bigler and Liben 2007; Katz 2003; Quintana 1998, 2007, 2008). Children's preferences are shaped by their effort to understand racial and cultural differences as they observe them and attend to messages they hear from family members, teachers, and others. To refer to preschoolers' behavior without acknowledging these characteristics and influences makes it difficult to understand why they occur as part of typical development. Understanding why these behaviors emerge developmentally is also important as families seek ways to encourage young children to be more cooperative, empathic, and accepting of human diversity. To help young children acquire desirable positive characteristics, adults must first understand why children develop as they do. The goal of these foundations is to help cultivate that understanding. The companion *California Preschool Curriculum Framework, Volume 3,* offers guidance on how teachers can be more effective in helping children learn about others and engage in cooperative and empathetic behavior.

Children form a remarkably diverse population. They vary in their temperamental qualities, personality, family background, cultural heritage and values, economic resources, family structure, and other ways. Children in California are especially diverse in their culture of origin. Culture is associated with family values and practices, language, and other characteristics that are directly related to the meaning of these foundations and their application to individual children, especially children who are English-language learners or from special populations (see, for example, Bowman and Moore 2006; Edwards and others 2006).

Although the developmental research on which these foundations are based is full of studies of English-speaking, middle-class European American children, there are fewer studies focused on children who speak other languages or come from other family, racial, or cultural backgrounds. Much more research of this kind is needed. In light of this limitation, the foundations are starting points for understanding young children's development and should be supplemented by the teacher's observations and understanding of individual children in preschool.

Likewise, more research is needed on the developmental advances described in these foundations for children with special needs, such as those with physical disabilities.

Taken together, these foundations describe developmental growth in understanding history and social sciences that is likely to be true of most preschoolers. Early childhood education program administrators, supervisors, and teachers must interpret them in light of their experience and knowledge of individual children and families in their programs, understanding the different strengths that children bring with them given their home experiences and the powerful influences of society (Banks 2006; Rogoff 1989). At times, it may be desirable to consult with outside experts for deeper understanding of children's backgrounds and what children bring from those experiences to the preschool setting.

Learning About History–Social Science

Finally, how should adults help young children acquire the essential lessons of civic participation, democracy, historical perspective, geographical awareness, culture, and a sense of self in a complex social world? The foundations are based on the assumption that young children develop understanding as they are encouraged to do so in everyday interactions with other children and adults (Mindes 2005). The best lessons in democracy, time sense, awareness of the natural and physical world, the marketplace, culture and diversity, responsible conduct, mutual respect, and self-understanding are those that are acquired as young children participate in carefully crafted experiences with teachers who encourage them not just through instruction, but also through guided participation in activities that strengthen developing awareness and understanding. The activities that nurture understanding in those areas are those involving extensive conversations between children and adults and between children and their peers; shared projects involving discovery and learning; and abundant play (Edwards and Ramsey 1986).

The most important purpose of these foundations is to help early childhood educators create environments and interactions that help young children understand themselves in a wonderfully expanding world.

Summary Table: History–Social Science Strands, Substrands, and Foundations

Strand	Substrand	Foundation
Self and Society	1.0 Culture and Diversity	1.1
	2.0 Relationships	2.1
	3.0 Social Roles and Occupations	3.1
Becoming a Preschool Community Member (Civics)	1.0 Skills for Democratic Participation	1.1
	2.0 Responsible Conduct	2.1
	3.0 Fairness and Respect for Other People	3.1
	4.0 Conflict Resolution	4.1
Sense of Time (History)	1.0 Understanding Past Events	1.1
	2.0 Anticipating and Planning Future Events	2.1
	3.0 Personal History	3.1
	4.0 Historical Changes in People and the World	4.1
Sense of Place (Geography and Ecology)	1.0 Navigating Familiar Locations	1.1
	2.0 Caring for the Natural World	2.1
	3.0 Understanding the Physical World Through Drawings and Maps	3.1
Marketplace (Economics)	1.0 Exchange	1.1

Self and Society

1.0 Culture and Diversity

At around 48 months of age	*At around 60 months of age*
1.1 Exhibit developing cultural, ethnic, and racial identity and understand relevant language and cultural practices. Display curiosity about diversity in human characteristics and practices, but prefer those of their own group.	**1.1** Manifest stronger cultural, ethnic, and racial identity and greater familiarity with relevant language, traditions, and other practices. Show more interest in human diversity, but strongly favor characteristics of their own group.
Examples	**Examples**
<ul><li>When parent leaves room during drop-off, child seeks a teacher assistant who speaks the child's home language.</li><li>Tells a Chinese American friend, "I can speak your language. *Ni hao* (Hello)!"</li><li>Shares with teacher, after a holiday weekend, "I helped make the tamales!"</li><li>Describes to a teacher the special foods her family ate at last night's Passover Seder.</li><li>Wants to touch Michiko's wheelchair.</li><li>Points to a child's sushi and asks, "What is that?" Shows interest in the response, but does not want to try it.</li><li>Points to a photo on the group's Family Board and says, "Tanisha looks like me."</li><li>While patting play dough, child tells a friend, "My *abuela* makes tortillas."</li></ul>	<ul><li>Proudly shares, "My mom can speak three languages: Cantonese, Vietnamese, and English!"</li><li>Learns and uses some simple words in a different language that is used by other children in the group.</li><li>Asks a new teacher, "Why do you always wear a scarf on your head?" and shows interest in the teacher's explanation.</li><li>Tells another girl, "You can't play if you have short hair. Only boys can have short hair."</li><li>While discussing their families, a child shares, "I'm half Mexican and half Salvadoran." Another child adds, "I'm half Japanese and half Jewish."</li><li>During a circle-time discussion of the holidays that families celebrate, suggests counting who celebrates Christmas, Hanukkah, and Chinese New Year.</li><li>Shares with teacher, "My name at school is Louis, but at home it is Young-Min Kim."</li><li>During music time, child tells group, "At the powwow, my sister did the fancy dance."</li><li>During lunch, asks another child, "Why don't you eat meat?"</li></ul>

2.0 Relationships

At around 48 months of age	At around 60 months of age
2.1 Interact comfortably with many peers and adults; actively contribute to creating and maintaining relationships with a few significant adults and peers.	**2.1** Understand the mutual responsibilities of relationships; take initiative in developing relationships that are mutual, cooperative, and exclusive.
Examples	**Examples**
• Seeks a special peer to sit with at circle time. • When hurt, seeks the assistance of a special teacher, even turning away from other adults who try to help. • Plays with a truck on the sand table alongside another child, and eventually the two children play together. • Goes to a particular teacher for comfort when having trouble separating from a family member during morning drop-off. • Plays with the same friend regularly; their play together is more cooperative and complex, but also more conflicted at times. • Notices when a friend or special teacher is absent, and asks about that person by name.	• Comes to the defense of a friend who is teased by another child. • Talks to a special teacher about a weekend activity that was exciting or scary. Responds to the teacher's description of her own weekend. • Works cooperatively with several friends to create a map of the outside play area, but does not include others who are not friends. • Shows another child who does not understand English what to do when the teacher says it is time to get ready for snack. • Asks a teacher for assistance in preparing to paint, cooperates with the teacher in getting ready, and describes the colors he or she will use. • Suggests taking turns with another child who also wants to bounce the large ball. • Seeks to play regularly with one or two friends, even to the extent of excluding other children who want to join in.

HISTORY–SOCIAL SCIENCE

3.0 Social Roles and Occupations

At around 48 months of age	*At around 60 months of age*
3.1 Play familiar adult social roles and occupations (such as parent, teacher, and doctor) consistent with their developing knowledge of these roles.	**3.1** Exhibit more sophisticated understanding of a broader variety of adult roles and occupations, but uncertain how work relates to income.
Examples	**Examples**
• Comments to a friend during pretend play, "I want to be the nurse and give these babies their flu shots like my mommy does." • Talks with children playing in the house area about who cooks dinner in his family. • Tells an adult that her mama "doesn't have time to do anything" because now she has to take care of the baby twins. • Watches with curiosity as a crew works from a high "bucket truck" to remove dead branches from a nearby tree. • Indicates, "Daddy's job is going to school."	• Shares with an adult that her mom now has to get up "really early" every day to get to her new job on time because she makes breakfast for other people. • Communicates that Papa has to work "extra hours" for a while, and he sometimes takes his supper to work in a lunchbox. • Comments that his mother is going to the bank to get some money. • Watches with interest and asks questions of Debbie, the plumber, while she fixes a sink faucet. • Tells other children in dramatic play area that mommies can be police officers, too, because girls can do what boys can do.

Becoming a Preschool Community Member (Civics)

1.0 Skills for Democratic Participation

At around 48 months of age	At around 60 months of age
1.1 Identify as members of a group, participate willingly in group activities, and begin to understand and accept responsibility as group members, although assistance is required in coordinating personal interests with those of others.	**1.1** Become involved as responsible participants in group activities, with growing understanding of the importance of considering others' opinions, group decision making, and respect for majority rules and the views of group members who disagree with the majority.
Examples	**Examples**
• Participates in an informal group vote about which song to sing, but sometimes protests or does not participate when the group's choice differs from hers.	• Communicates, "Let's vote!" when the group is divided about which song to sing.
• Responds appropriately by putting away materials when the teacher indicates that it is time for cleanup, although may need guidance about what to do.	• Anticipates the predictable routines of the day, such as initiating lunchtime handwashing, without being prompted.
• Shares an idea or opinion, sometimes by responding enthusiastically to others' ideas, and can attend to the comments and ideas of others for a short while, sometimes with adult prompting.	• Suggests doing both activities when children are divided about what to do next.
• Helps create rules that contribute to a safe and harmonious environment and can usually follow them with adult reminders.	• Organizes or participates with a group of friends to play particular roles during dramatic play in the housekeeping area.
• When a friend wants to touch the goldfish in the fish tank, tells the friend, "No touching the fish. It's the rule!"	• When frustrated with children who are disrupting his group's game, indicates to a teacher that they are not following the rules.
	• Follows the different sets of rules at home and at school.
	• Uses vocabulary for making and discussing rules (*vote, decide, compromise*).
	• Explains the reasons for some rules (e.g., why hitting other people is not allowed).

2.0 Responsible Conduct

At around 48 months of age	At around 60 months of age
2.1 Strive to cooperate with group expectations to maintain adult approval and get along with others. Self-control is inconsistent, however, especially when children are frustrated or upset.	**2.1** Exhibit responsible conduct more reliably as children develop self-esteem (and adult approval) from being responsible group members. May also manage others' behavior to ensure that others also fit in with group expectations.
Examples	**Examples**
• Contributes to group routines, such as cleanup, but can easily be distracted while doing so.	• Begins to gather materials for an art project without being reminded by the teacher.
• Plays cooperatively with other children but may act aggressively when frustrated by another's behavior.	• Tells another child to put away blocks when snack time is announced, indicating that cleaning up before eating is a rule.
• Seeks the teacher's acknowledgment after acting helpfully.	• Cleans up a spill on her own, without being asked to do so.
• Is pleased to be given a "helper" role, such as feeding a pet or watering the plants.	• Willingly helps with tasks that he notices need to be done (such as getting more paper towels).
• Agrees to share a large tub of building materials with another child when given time to adjust to the idea.	• Shares her play dough, without prompting, when another child wants to join in.
• Seeks help from an adult when a friend is injured while playing outside.	• Tells a teacher when another child is not following a group rule.
	• Expresses anger toward another child by using language instead of physical aggression.

3.0 Fairness and Respect for Other People

At around 48 months of age	*At around 60 months of age*
3.1 Respond to the feelings and needs of others with simple forms of assistance, sharing, and turn-taking. Understand the importance of rules that protect fairness and maintain order.	**3.1** Pay attention to others' feelings, more likely to provide assistance, and try to coordinate personal desires with those of other children in mutually satisfactory ways. Actively support rules that protect fairness to others.
Examples	**Examples**
• With the teacher's prompting, shares the blocks she is using with another child who wants to use them. • Understands the importance of putting toys away in their proper places to maintain order; appreciates that it is even more important to be nice to others. • Realizes, after an adult's explanation of the situation, that his disruption of a table game is the reason another child is angry at him. • Indicates, "That's not fair!" when a friend's interests are ignored or another child is excluded. • Notices a new child crying after the child's mother has left and offers a favorite toy to help the child feel better.	• Tells a teacher, "Akito is sad because she wanted to play with Emma" and problem-solves with the teacher about how to help. • Helps a friend rebuild a sandcastle that has collapsed. • Suggests taking turns with several children who want to get on the swing. • While playing in the dramatic play area, agrees to use another child's ideas about what to cook for a family celebration.

HISTORY–SOCIAL SCIENCE

4.0 Conflict Resolution

At around 48 months of age	*At around 60 months of age*
4.1 Can use simple bargaining strategies and seek adult assistance when in conflict with other children or adults, although frustration, distress, or aggression also occurs.	**4.1** More capable of negotiating, compromising, and finding cooperative means of resolving conflict with peers or adults, although verbal aggression may also result.
Examples	**Examples**
• When two children want to use the same tricycle, one indicates to the other, "You can use it after I'm done." • Teacher announces cleanup time; one child agrees to put away her puzzle as soon as she finishes it. • Seeks help from the teacher when another child takes the trucks he was using in the sandbox. • Cries when a peer does not let him play with some of the animal figures, but offers solutions to the problem when a teacher guides both children in discussion.	• Waits for a turn at the swings, indicating with gestures that she is waiting to swing. • When two children want to use the same tricycle, one suggests that they take turns. • When a teacher cautions a child about running indoors, the child begins to walk fast instead. • Indicates, "We need another one!" to the teacher when commenting that children always want to wear the one green shirt in the dramatic play area. • Communicates to a peer, "There's only room for two people in here so you can't play with us." • Reminds another child of the rule about washing hands before mealtime or shows by example.

Sense of Time (History)

1.0 Understanding Past Events

At around 48 months of age	At around 60 months of age
1.1 Recall past experiences easily and enjoy hearing stories about the past, but require adult help to determine when past events occurred in relation to each other and to connect them with current experience.	**1.1** Show improving ability to relate past events to other past events and current experiences, although adult assistance continues to be important.
Examples	**Examples**
• Describes a family trip for the teacher, but is unable to describe when the trip occurred. • When a teacher asks what other countries the children have visited, one child answers, "Philippines! I have lots of cousins there." • Although his birthday was a month ago, he describes looking forward to his birthday, which he tells an adult "is coming soon." • While in the yard, looks under bushes for a caterpillar seen the day before. • Often refers to anything done in the past as "yesterday." • A foster child shares with the teacher, "I used to live in a home with lots of kids, and now I live with a family where I'm the only one." • Announces that her mom had a little baby boy and that he will be little for a long, long time.	• Is happy and explains that it is because his daddy arrived home yesterday from a long trip. • Two girls recall, with a teacher, that the school garden plants died because they did not receive enough water when the weather became hot. • Asks a teacher if she is feeling better today because he missed her when she was sick yesterday. • Tells a friend that she used to share a bedroom with her sister, but she does not anymore because her sister is "all grown up and married now." • When asked about weekend activities, shares that he and his mom went to the post office to mail a big package to grandparents in Mexico. • Shares that she is sad because her cousins just moved away and now they will not be together every day. • Arranges pictures to indicate the time sequence in the context of events in a story (e.g., *The Little Red Hen, The Very Hungry Caterpillar*).

2.0   Anticipating and Planning Future Events

At around 48 months of age	At around 60 months of age
2.1 Anticipate events in familiar situations in the near future, with adult assistance.	**2.1** Distinguish when future events will happen, plan for them, and make choices (with adult assistance) that anticipate future needs.
Examples	**Examples**
• When the teacher points to the art photo in the picture schedule, the child begins to prepare (putting on an apron, moving paper to the easel). • When asked what he is going to do tomorrow, indicates that he will have breakfast and then come to school. • Tells an adult, "When we go outside, I need a plastic bag on my cast so it won't get muddy." • Tells other children that she and her papa go outside to look at the stars when it gets dark, right after they eat dinner. • Knows, with the help of a picture schedule, that snack time at preschool always follows circle time. • Excitedly tells the teacher, "We're going to the airport to pick up my uncle from Taiwan next week!" but has no idea how soon next week will be. • At planning time, a child who is nonverbal uses a communication board with pictures to indicate where he will play first. • When asked for an idea about what the group will need to bring on a lunchtime picnic, suggests a blanket.	• As the group gets ready to go on a trip to the fire station, asks the teacher whether they should bring the firefighter's hat from the dress-up area. • Tells a friend that she has to give away toys to make room for her grandparents from India, who will be coming to live with her. • Because of a special event, the day's schedule is changed. Several children express concern that snack time will be skipped. • Communicates to a friend, "Next time we go to the zoo, I will have my electric wheelchair, so I can keep up with you." • Tells teacher, "I get to visit my cousins on Saturday. Mommy says that's after two more sleeps!" • Encourages friend to put on his shoes and jacket fast so they will have more time to dig in the sandbox together. • When the nurse enters, a child tells her friend that it is time for a tube feeding and that she will come back to play in 10 minutes. • Knowing that park time is at 10:00 every day, brings jacket from cubby and asks, "Is it 10:00 yet?"

HISTORY–SOCIAL SCIENCE

3.0 Personal History

At around 48 months of age	*At around 60 months of age*
3.1 Proudly display developing skills to attract adult attention and share simple accounts about recent experiences.	**3.1** Compare current abilities with skills at a younger age and share more detailed autobiographical stories about recent experiences.
Examples	**Examples**
• Shows a teacher his drawing of a cat and smiles when the teacher says, "Look at your cat's long tail and whiskers!" • Tells a teacher how Grandma made rice for breakfast this morning. • Exclaims, "Now I can run fast! My brother says he can't catch me!" • Strives to imitate the actions and skills of older children. • Tells an adult that he helped Papa fix the table leg last night. • Communicates at the park, "Look, Ms. Martinez, I can slide all by myself now because I am a big girl."	• Tells a teacher that she is now strong enough to help her mom carry bags home from the market and then recalls some things they brought home last night. • Shares with other children that he was once little and that soon they will be big like him. • Names all the family members who came to her house on Sunday to celebrate her grandpa's birthday. • After falling and scraping a knee, comments that it hurts a little, but not as much as last time. • Tells a teacher that she is teaching her baby sister how to walk and recounts that when she was a baby she only crawled, too, but that now she can even run and jump.

HISTORY–SOCIAL SCIENCE

HISTORY–SOCIAL SCIENCE

4.0 Historical Changes in People and the World

At around 48 months of age	*At around 60 months of age*
4.1 Easily distinguish older family members from younger ones (and other people) and events in the recent past from those that happened "long ago," although do not readily sequence historical events on a timeline.	**4.1** Develop an interest in family history (e.g., when family members were children) as well as events of "long ago," and begin to understand when these events occurred in relation to each other.
Examples	**Examples**
• Builds castles with blocks but is not aware of, or interested in, when these structures were built historically. • Can readily identify people who are very young or very old. • Thinks of fairy tale characters, as well as science fiction superheroes, as being real but simply not here right now.	• Can identify, with adult assistance, the relative ages of family members (e.g., grandparents, parents, siblings, self). • Tells a teacher that when her grandma and grandpa were little they lived in Mexico, but when they grew up, they moved here. • Shares with her teacher, "My baby brother was born last week and I was born a long time ago—almost five years!" • Says, "My mommy came from Guatemala a long time ago!" when the teacher asks where children's families came from. • Understands that dinosaurs lived long ago and that Grandpa was a boy long ago, but cannot distinguish how long ago these events occurred.

Sense of Place (Geography and Ecology)

1.0 Navigating Familiar Locations

At around 48 months of age	*At around 60 months of age*
1.1 Identify the characteristics of familiar locations such as home and school, describe objects and activities associated with each, recognize the routes between them, and begin using simple directional language (with various degrees of accuracy).	**1.1** Comprehend larger familiar locations, such as the characteristics of their community and region (including hills and streams, weather, common activities) and the distances between familiar locations (such as between home and school), and compare their home community with those of others.
Examples	**Examples**
• Understands that home is where one sleeps at night and gets dressed in the morning. • Demonstrates knowledge that preschool environments have reading areas with books. • Asks as mother is driving to preschool, "Are we going to school?" • When asked by an adult, "Where is the sand table?" the child replies, "over there" while gesturing in the general direction. • When riding with other people, excitedly shouts, "That's my school!" and talks about the people and activities there. • Shares with a teacher, "Sam is my friend. He lives next door." • Directs an adult's attention to a wildlife poster by indicating that it is "over" the sink.	• Indicates that everybody needs a raincoat where he lives. • Tells a teacher, "My grandpa lives where it gets real cold in the winter, much colder than here. It even snows!" • Knows that her cousins live far away because it takes a long time to get to her cousin's house by car. • Explains, "On the way to school, we have to walk up two gigantic hills" and describes excitedly what that is like. • When the teacher leads children to take a new route on the way back from an outdoor trip, communicates "No, this way!" • Excitedly tells a teacher that she just saw some monarch caterpillars on her way to school ("On the bushes next to the river").

HISTORY-SOCIAL SCIENCE

2.0 Caring for the Natural World

At around 48 months of age	*At around 60 months of age*
2.1 Show an interest in nature (including animals, plants, and weather) especially as children experience it directly. Begin to understand human interactions with the environment (such as pollution in a lake or stream) and the importance of taking care of plants and animals.	**2.1** Show an interest in a wider range of natural phenomena, including those outside direct experience (such as snow for a child living in Southern California), and are more concerned about caring for the natural world and the positive and negative impacts of people on the natural world (e.g., recycling, putting trash in trash cans).
Examples	**Examples**
• Contributes to circle-time discussion of the day's weather, readily describing it as hot, cold, rainy, and so forth. • Checks the plant pots on the windowsill daily after watering them to find out whether the seeds have started to grow. • Turns over big rocks on the playground to see if there are worms or bugs underneath, but is careful not to squish them. • One child's father brings the family's pet kitten to circle time, and the child tells everyone how to hold and pet the kitten carefully so it will feel safe and not get hurt. • On a nature hike, points to litter and asks, "Who did this?"	• Shares with a teacher that it snows where his cousins live and no flowers are outside because it is too cold for them to grow. • Finds a broken brown eggshell outdoors and communicates that he hopes the bird is okay. • Communicates to other children that her family recycles cans and bottles to care for the natural environment. • Tells a teacher that Mommy does not like plastic bags because they are bad for the environment. • When outside on a walk, picks up litter and throws it into a trash can. • After looking at a book about bears, expresses interest in polar bears and asks the teacher where they live.

3.0 Understanding the Physical World Through Drawings and Maps

At around 48 months of age	At around 60 months of age
3.1 Can use drawings, globes, and maps to refer to the physical world, although often unclear on the use of map symbols.	**3.1** Create their own drawings, maps, and models; are more skilled at using globes, maps, and map symbols; and use maps for basic problem solving (such as locating objects) with adult guidance.
Examples	**Examples**
• Finds a crumpled piece of paper with scribbled lines on it and decides that it is a map to buried treasure. • In describing a drawing to an adult, gestures to a square that she calls her house and explains that the zigzag lines in front of it are where she rode her tricycle yesterday. • Looking at an adult map, can identify lines, with an adult's help, that represent roads and green areas indicating farmland, but has difficulty interpreting other map symbols.	• Builds a landscape on the sand table and move cars and trucks on the roads she has created. • Draws a map of the outside play area, indicating to an adult the location of trees, climbing structures, and buildings. • After looking at a road map, is surprised that it takes so long to drive to the destination because it did not look far away on the map.

HISTORY–SOCIAL SCIENCE

Marketplace (Economics)

1.0 Exchange

At around 48 months of age	*At around 60 months of age*
1.1 Understand ownership, limited supply, what stores do, give-and-take, and payment of money to sellers. Show interest in money and its function, but still figuring out the relative value of coins.	**1.1** Understand more complex economic concepts (e.g., bartering; more money is needed for things of greater value; if more people want something, more will be sold).
Examples	**Examples**
• Agrees to give another child two plastic oranges if the child will give her two pennies.	• Tells a friend that her family needs a new car, but they need lots of money first.
• Wheels to the grocery store in the dramatic play area and asks, "Who wants to buy some tamales?"	• Makes a sign in the pretend shoe store indicating that small shoes cost $1 and big shoes cost $2.
• Cuts a small rectangle out of cardboard at the art table and indicates that it is his credit card.	• Several children create clay animal sculptures and decide to trade them with each other.
• Two friends dress up in the house area to go shopping, filling their wallets with play money.	• Explains to a teacher, "We don't have enough money to just get whatever we want at the store."
• Asks another child, "Will you give me a haircut? I'll pay you some money."	• Suggests to a teacher that there is "too much stuff" in the room and that they should have a sale.
• Reminds another child, "Don't take Carlo's jacket from his cubby!"	• When a peer in the dramatic play area suggests making sandwiches to sell, says, "No, let's make a pizza store, because everyone wants to buy pizza!"
• Rushes outside to ride favorite tricycle, knowing that it is a popular toy.	• While playing with a plastic horse, tells a friend, "Having a real horse of my own costs too much money."
• Looks forward to going to a familiar grocery store to buy things.	

Bibliographic Notes

Self and Society

Culture and Diversity

As preschoolers develop a sense of self, the cultural, ethnic, and racial identity that they share with family members becomes a more important part of their self-awareness (Aboud 1984, 1987; Bennett and Sani 2008; Edwards and Ramsey 1986; Katz 2003; Quintana 1998). In the late preschool years, children begin to appreciate—and take pride in—the language, traditions, foods, arts, literature, and other practices associated with this identity. In a sense, as their understanding of their cultural, ethnic, and racial membership expands, it becomes incorporated into their sense of who they are.

At the same time, preschoolers become more interested in the beliefs, behaviors, and lives of other people who live in "faraway places." Their understanding of the geographical vastness of the world expands in the fourth and fifth years, and their interest in human diversity grows. The result is fascination (and, at times, amazement) with the appearance, practices, languages, traditions, and arts of people around the world. Preschoolers take an interest in the lives of people who live nearby who are different from them—such as children who look different from themselves, who speak different languages, have different abilities, and come from different socioeconomic and cultural communities. As preschoolers understand the characteristics of their own identity better, they become more interested in people who are different from them.

Preschoolers are quick to compare and contrast others' characteristics with their own, of course, and readily prefer the characteristics of their own group membership (Aboud 1988, 2003, 2008; Barbarin and Odom 2009; Bigler and Liben 2007; Katz 2003; Quintana 1998, 2007, 2008). Social scientists call this behavior **in-group bias** (terms in bold are defined in the Glossary), which is apparent at age four and increases as young children reach ages five and six. There has been some debate about whether an in-group bias is as apparent in certain groups of young children, about which the evidence is mixed (see Quintana 2007, 2008). As young children consolidate their own sense of themselves and the groups (e.g., gender, cultural, racial) that are part of their identity, they increasingly value characteristics of the groups with which they identify. Children who favor their own cultural, ethnic, and racial group may seem to be negative toward other groups; however, it primarily means that children are *more* likely to favor people who resemble them, whose characteristics are more familiar and comfortable to them (Aboud 2003; Quintana 2008). This bias strengthens as children enter the early primary grades and then weakens with increasing age in the primary grades as children become more interested in differences and more comfortable with their own identity.

These findings have led to an interest in understanding why preferential biases for one's own culture, ethnicity,

HISTORY–SOCIAL SCIENCE

and race emerge in early childhood and how to create more accepting attitudes in preschoolers. Research has focused on how children acquire biases and stereotypes from their family members; some studies find that by age five, children are familiar with basic, concrete racial stereotypes (Aboud 1988; Brown and Bigler 2005). In addition, researchers have also focused on how race and ethnicity are, for young children, based on visible physical characteristics that naturally leads to the categorization of people by race and, in turn, the assignment of positive or negative characteristics on the basis of this physical feature (Hirschfeld 2008; Quintana 2008).

Young children may thus perceive race as a core, essential quality of individuals that leads to many other characteristics and behaviors rather than perceiving race as just one of many differences between people (Hirschfeld 1996). Moreover, because many young children have limited direct exposure to people of different cultures, ethnicities, and races, lack of familiarity tends to maintain—if not create—positive in-group biases.

Therefore, a preschool with cultural, racial, and linguistic diversity is a benefit to young children, especially if teachers purposefully draw attention to and value this diversity in their practices. Early childhood education programs that promote accepting attitudes toward cultural, ethnic, and racial differences among young children have focused on increasing children's exposure to the diversity of local cultures, ethnicities, and races in the community; improving perspective taking and **pro-social** attitudes; and changing the messages that children receive from teachers and families (see,

for example, Barbarin and Odom 2009; Bigler and Liben 2007). Although their in-group bias has many developmental origins, young children benefit substantially from an early childhood education setting where diversity is prized and other people are appreciated for their differences.

Relationships

Developing relationships with other adults and children is one of the most important challenges in an early childhood education program. In contrast to family relationships, preschoolers must exercise greater social skill to develop and maintain relationships with others in the program, which stretches their capacities for social interaction. This is especially true for peer relationships, because other preschoolers are much less generous social partners than are most adults (Rubin, Bukowski, and Parker 2006; Rubin and others 2005).

During the period from ages three to five, preschoolers make considerable progress in their skills for developing and maintaining satisfying relationships with teachers and peers (Berlin, Cassidy, and Appleyard 2008; Dunn 1993; Hartup 1996; Howes and Spieker 2008; Parker and Gottman 1989; Shonkoff and Phillips 2000). The majority of older three-year-olds have developed social skills for doing so, including developing abilities to engage in simple conversations, participate in shared activities, cooperate with requests or instructions, and ask (adults) for help when needed. The skills constitute a foundation for developing friendships with one or two peers and close relationships with one or two special teachers whom the child seeks for shared activity, assistance, and acknowledgment of accomplishments. By the time children are at the end of their fourth year, these skills have expanded because the child has advanced significantly in social understanding, particularly in the capacity to view relationships as mutual and reciprocal rather than one-sided.

The cognitive flexibility to appreciate that another person's needs and interests in a relationship must be recognized enables five-year-olds to develop relationships that are more mutual, cooperative, and helpful. They are more likely to suggest turn-taking when more than one child wants to use the same toy, to work together with several children on a project, and to spontaneously share paints, toys, or food with another child or adult. Children of this age are more likely to show an interest in the other child's experiences or ask a teacher what she did during the weekend (after the teacher has inquired about the child's weekend). They are also more likely to work cooperatively for an extended period with friends and special teachers, although they may also seek to make these relationships more exclusive than do younger children. Exclusive relationships may mean other children who wish to join in will be rejected.

Children who are English learners or who have disabilities may face special challenges in the development of close relationships with teachers and peers. Trusting, secure relationships with teachers—especially when teachers speak the language of the child's home environment—can be especially important in helping English learners to feel comfortable and welcome and to find their place in the peer social environment. For children who have physical disabilities, the teacher–child relationship can be important to strengthening self-confidence and negotiating relationships with peers (Thompson and Thompson 2010).

The quality of young children's relationships with early childhood education teachers and peers is important to school readiness (Thompson 2002; Thompson and Raikes 2007). Several studies have reported that the warmth and security of the preschool child's relationship with the teacher are predictive of the child's subsequent academic performance, attentional skills, and social competence in the kindergarten and primary-grades classroom (Bowman, Donovan, and Burns 2001; Lamb 1998; Peisner-Feinberg and others 2001; Pianta, Nimetz, and Bennett 1997).

Furthermore, the importance of developing relationship skills is underscored by other findings that once children have entered school, the quality of the teacher–child relationship and the amount of conflict in that relationship are predictive of children's poorer academic performance and greater behavior problems in the classroom, sometimes years later (Birch and Ladd 1997; Hamre and Pianta 2001; La Paro and Pianta 2000; Pianta, Steinberg, and Rollins 1995; Pianta and Stuhlman 2004a, 2004b).

Other studies show that friendships with peers are important to a child's transition to school, as successful peer relationships contribute to better school adjustment. Friendships at school cause kindergarten and primary-grades children to look forward to attending school, to have a more positive classroom experience, and to achieve more as students (Ladd, Kochenderfer, and Coleman 1996, 1997; Ladd, Birch, and Buhs 1999).

Relationship skills are important to both citizenship and school success.

Social Roles and Occupations

As their view of themselves and the social world expands, preschoolers become fascinated by the adult roles (e.g., parent, grandparent, neighbor) and occupations (e.g., teacher, firefighter, bus driver, doctor) with which they are familiar (Edwards and Ramsey 1986). This greater interest develops both from their expanding exploration of the world around them and their interest in imagining the roles they might assume when they grow up. This interest can be observed most readily in young children's pretend play—when they take on familiar adult social roles (e.g., parent, police officer), imagined adult roles (e.g., superhero, princess), and other roles (e.g., child, baby) in the context of the pretend-play scripts they create (Howes 1992). But their interest in adult social roles and occupations may also be observed in their delight in taking a trip to the fire station, watching a custodian work on the plumbing, seeing the gardener plant a shrub, or through other opportunities to directly observe an adult in work-related activity.

Their developing understanding of adult social roles and occupations does not yet encompass, however, the broader significance of these jobs. More specifically, even five-year-olds do not yet understand the connection between adult work and family income: that adults work in order to earn the income by which the family lives. Instead, preschoolers understand an adult's job as simply what that person does, and this is differentiated from how adults get money by going to a bank (Berti and Bombi 1988; Burris

1983). Children have a limited understanding of the economy and perceive financial matters primarily in terms of the consumer, not the worker, and it means that preschoolers are unlikely to appreciate the work-related circumstances that can influence family economic well-being, such as what happens when an adult is unable to work for a period of time, has reduced hours, or experiences a furlough.

Becoming a Preschool Community Member (Civics)

Skills for Democratic Participation

For most preschoolers, the early childhood education program is the first social setting in which skills of citizenship can be learned, understood, and practiced. This is where teachers actively strive to involve children in citizenship and democratic skills, such as helping to create and support group rules and expectations, group decision making (such as voting), valuing the expression of opinions and respect for others' opinions, and understanding the importance of recognizing the majority's judgment but also respecting minority views. These are, of course, the foundations of democratic society in the everyday practices of the preschool program.

For young children, participation as a group citizen is challenging because it requires several skills that are emerging during this period: awareness of others' feelings and desires and the growing ability to coordinate others' interests with one's own; emerging capacities for self-regulation and self-control (especially when participating in group activities that are not personally interesting or desirable); memory skills for recalling group rules and expectations and spontaneously applying them to one's own conduct; and developing self-awareness that contributes to the young child's self-identification as a group member and not just as an individual. Fortunately, many of these core capacities are developing significantly during the preschool years (see Bronson 2000; Calkins and Williford 2009; Harris 2006; Harter 1999, 2006; Thompson 2006; Thompson and Goodman 2009). By the end of the fourth year and early in the fifth year, young children understand others' views and group expectations well enough to be cooperative participants as group members. By the end of the fifth year, they are also capable of being active contributors to democratic processes.

Emerging "citizenship" involves participation in democratic processes, which for preschoolers involves group discussion, expressing and listening to opinions, group decision making, and abiding by the majority view while also respecting minority interests. Citizenship skills are particularly challenging for young children who are still learning the dominant language and cultural practices of the preschool setting and may be at a disadvantage as a result of language and a more limited sense of participation. Sometimes lack of participation in the group is due to linguistic and cultural barriers more than disinterest, and teachers can support emerging citizenship by purposefully ensuring that each child's cultural and linguistic background is valued.

The skills of group membership are challenging for all young children, whose emotional devotion to their own preferences and emerging self-regulatory capacities may make it difficult for them to attend carefully to contrary viewpoints and accept a majority decision that runs against personal preferences. Teachers can support these developing citizenship skills by modeling these practices (e.g., acknowledging the value of an opinion that is contrary to the teacher's own), enlisting children's identification as a group (e.g., describing the preschool setting as "our" place), enlisting the group in brainstorming and collective problem solving, and acknowledging the disappointment of not getting one's way (Edwards and Ramsey 1986; Thompson and Twibell 2009). These are important practices because for young children, emerging citizenship skills are learned through their guided enactment rather than through verbal instruction alone. In other words, young children learn about a democratic society by participating in a democracy.

Responsible Conduct

Research on the development of early responsible conduct in young children has shown that preschoolers are motivated to act responsibly for several reasons (Kochanska and Thompson 1997; Thompson, Meyer, and McGinley 2006). First, they act cooperatively to earn an adult's approval, which is an early and strong incentive for responsible conduct. Striving for an adult's praise and commendation is one reason that young children seek an adult's attention for their good behavior. Second, they act cooperatively because it contributes to self-esteem and the sense of being a "good" boy or girl and responsible group member. Third, they act cooperatively out of concern for others' feelings and needs. This can be seen especially when young children act helpfully to someone who has been hurt or needs assistance. Fourth, young children act cooperatively to avoid negative consequences, such as disapproval or failure to comply with an adult's instructions or rules.

Although cooperating to avoid disapproval and punishment has traditionally been emphasized in moral development theories, new research shows that the other incentives discussed above may influence young children even more than commonly believed. For example, two studies have shown that early responsible conduct is more strongly influenced by a mother's comments about others' feelings and needs than by the frequency with which she warns about rules and the consequences of breaking them (Laible and Thompson 2000, 2002; see also Kochanska and Thompson 1997; Thompson, Meyer, and McGinley 2006). The same is likely to be true of the early childhood education program. When a teacher emphasizes the impact of inappropriate conduct on others and others' feelings more than the negative consequences of breaking a rule, it provides a stronger foundation for helpful, constructive behavior in the future.

The major obstacle to responsible conduct in preschoolers is not egocentrism but limitations in their capacities for self-regulation, especially when they are frustrated or upset. Fortunately, young children acquire greater skills in managing their impulses, feelings, and behavior from three to five years of age (see Calkins and Williford 2009; Thompson 1990, 1994). Young

children's emerging capacities for self-control can be enlisted to support responsible conduct when teachers are careful to ensure that their expectations for children are developmentally appropriate; the program environment is organized to reduce conflict (e.g., there are sufficient play materials for children); and teachers help children understand and remember group expectations, put into words their angry feelings, and help them devise appropriate ways of resolving conflict when they are frustrated (Edwards and Ramsey 1986; Thompson and Twibell 2009). Children can also be helped by external cues, such as pictures, drawings, and other means of prompting desired behavior (Carta and others 2000).

Teachers should be especially sensitive to the frustration and impediments to self-regulation encountered by children from culturally or linguistically diverse backgrounds, children who have disabilities or other special needs, or those who may not be able to fully participate in the group for other reasons. Difficult behavior may be manifested because of these feelings of being excluded more than from an unwillingness to cooperate. Teachers can be helpful by ensuring that these children receive the support necessary to be competent, participating members of the community.

Fairness and Respect for Other People

By the age of three, children can accurately interpret the feelings of other people and can distinguish them from their own feelings. Moreover, children of this age already have a basic understanding of why others might feel as they do (Denham 1998, 2006; Harris 1989, 2006; Thompson 2006; Thompson, Goodvin, and Meyer 2006; Thompson and Lagattuta 2006). In the years that follow, young children build on this nonegocentric awareness by learning how to respond appropriately to the feelings and needs of other people. This can be challenging for young children for two reasons. First, they must figure out how to respond in a way that is appropriate to what another child feels or wants (e.g., "What will make Maria feel better right now?"). Second, when another child's desires conflict with the child's own— such as when they both want to play with the same train—they must figure out how to cooperate in a manner that can satisfy both children. Each of these skills is important to developing a sense of fairness and respect for other people, and they are central to developing social competence, especially with peers (Howes 1987, 1988).

Young children also begin to construct an understanding of standards of conduct. Researchers have shown that as young as age three, children distinguish between two kinds of standards (Smetana 1981, 1985; Smetana and Braeges 1990). The first are **moral standards** that are based on young children's awareness of other people's feelings and needs. Moral standards include simple prohibitions such as that it is wrong to hurt others or steal from another person. The second are **social conventional standards** that are intended to maintain social order. Examples include expectations about putting away toys in their proper places, sitting in the right place for circle time, and cleaning up after meals. By age four, young children under-

stand that moral rules are more serious because they are based on human welfare (Thompson, Meyer, and McGinley 2006; Smetana 1981, 1985).

For children near their fourth birthday, an adult's assistance is especially important in helping to clarify another person's feelings and needs and determine how to respond appropriately. In doing so, teachers can put the other person's feelings and desires into words and suggest how the child might respond. Children nearer their fifth birthday have greater knowledge of people's feelings. For this reason, they are also more capable of providing help and thinking of ways in which the needs and interests of different people can be cooperatively coordinated.

Conflict Resolution

Conflict with a peer or a teacher's request is a common preschool experience, but it also presents opportunities for the development of social understanding. Nothing focuses a young child's mind on what another person is thinking or feeling more than the realization that conflict with that person must be resolved. The period of three to five years of age is one of significant growth in conflict resolution because preschoolers are advancing in their understanding of others' feelings, intentions, and desires. Preschoolers are developing the cognitive flexibility to balance an awareness of another person's intentions with their own desires (Fabes and Eisenberg 1992). For three-year-olds, peer conflict is likely to result in distress, physical aggression, or adult mediation or assistance. By the fourth birthday, these remain likely outcomes but are supplemented by the young child's

HISTORY–SOCIAL SCIENCE

developing capacity to bargain in simple ways, such as offering to comply with a teacher's request after the child has finished a desired activity or to let another child have a turn with a toy after a few minutes. These bargaining strategies reflect a dawning recognition of the other person's desires or needs and an effort to find a solution that satisfies both the child and the other person. This reflects a significant advance in psychological understanding as well as growth in the capacity to work cooperatively with other people.

By the end of the fifth year, the child's ability to understand another's point of view has advanced further, enabling more sophisticated approaches to conflict resolution that result in satisfactory solutions for both children. With peers and teachers, these include negotiation and compromise in ways that recognize the other person's needs as well as the child's own. To be sure, older four- and five-year-olds are not likely to suggest good solutions consistently (their proposals for compromise are likely to be driven by self-interest), and further negotiation is likely to be needed. Additionally, a five-year-old's conflict-resolution skills do not mean that distress, physical aggression, verbal aggression, and taunting may not also arise, especially during conflict with peers. But the capacity for negotiated conflict resolution means that children of this age have a foundation of social understanding that teachers can rely on to help children use compromise more frequently in their encounters with others. Children who have difficulty expressing themselves in English may need special teacher support in these situations.

Sense of Time (History)

Understanding Past Events

The preschool years are a period of major advance in young children's understanding of past, present, and future and the association between these events in time. As for past events, children in their fourth year can readily describe events in the recent and distant past (such as what they did yesterday or their birthday party several weeks ago), but this ability may cause adults to overestimate children's understanding of time sequences. For example, children around 48 months have difficulty locating past events in relation to one another, such as understanding whether their last birthday preceded the Fourth of July celebration or followed it if the two were close in time or occurred long ago (Friedman 1991, 1992; Friedman, Gardner, and Zubin 1995; Friedman and Kemp 1998). Young children's memory of events is not the continuous timeline that it is for adults; instead, it consists of recollections of particular events that are isolated "islands in time" that may not be well connected to other past events (Friedman 2005). Furthermore, young children may also confuse events in the recent past and the near future, such as describing a Valentine's Day that has just passed as an event to come (Friedman 2003). They also have difficulty connecting past events to present experience without adult assistance.

Older preschoolers are somewhat more skilled in locating past events in relation to each other and in distinguishing how far in the past certain events took place. In addition, they have a better understanding of how past events can influence the present, such as knowing how yesterday's birthday party can make someone feel happy today (Povinelli 1995, 2001; Povinelli, Landau, and Perilloux 1996; Povinelli and others 1999; Povinelli and Simon 1998). These skills provide a foundation that helps young children make connections between past events and current feelings, beliefs, and skills and also contribute to the growth of autobiographical memory (discussed later in relation to personal history).

Research studies show that young children's sense of time is strengthened when adults use predictable routines that children can incorporate into their **mental "scripts"** of everyday events (e.g., Nelson 2001). Furthermore, research shows that conversations with adults—in which adults help children understand the connections between past events and current experience and remind children of when those past events took place—help young children develop these skills (Fivush 2001; Nelson 2001).

There are also important cultural differences in how **narrative practices** —that is, different ways of telling stories, such as how much detail is included or whether explanations are provided—contribute to young children's sense of the past, present, and future. Some families emphasize linear time sequences (i.e., telling about the first thing that happened, followed by the second thing, followed by the third thing, and so on). Others use emotional cues (i.e., excitement, joy, amazement, sadness, fear, or anger of the characters in response to different parts of a story) as the connections between different events in time. Still others use different practices based on cultural background (Aukrust and Snow 1998; Leyva and others 2008; Melzi and Caspe 2005). Narrative practices are important because they contribute to the development of young children's sense of time and cues used for making connections between different events. Knowledge of these practices can be important for teachers in their use of narrative stories and shared recollection with young children.

Understanding of past events develops significantly after the preschool years. Children become more skilled at relating past events to each other by using time markers (such as "last fall" or "last Wednesday") to help them recall certain past events, understanding time sequences (e.g., a beach trip probably occurred during the summer), and comprehending the typical order of recurring events (e.g., Thanksgiving always comes before Christmas). Older children and adults are also aware that memories of recent events are much more vivid and clear than are memories of events from long ago. This understanding also contributes to proper sequencing. Taken together, a variety of cognitive skills are involved in understanding past events, and preschoolers are only beginning to acquire those skills. For this reason, although they are delighted to talk about past events with an interested adult, they may have a surprisingly limited sense of the past.

Anticipating and Planning Future Events

Thinking about future events is a cognitive challenge for young children because it requires imagining what will happen in an uncertain future (in contrast to past events, which are real because they actually happened). Despite this, children around 48 months are able to describe what will happen in the near future—later in the day or tomorrow—especially when they can predict on the basis of familiar, well-established, daily routines. For example, four-year-olds can describe what will happen next in the daily routine—cleanup and then snack time—and also the events of the next day when they are based on a familiar routine (Busby and Suddendorf 2005). However, just as they have difficulty sequencing events of the past, four-year-olds also have difficulty distinguishing events that will occur soon from those that will occur later and those that will occur in the distant future.

At age five, children are more skilled in sequencing and distinguishing events (Friedman 2000, 2002, 2003). Thus five-year-olds are beginning to create an adultlike view of the future that accurately distinguishes how soon future events will happen. Children of this age are also more capable of planning appropriately for future events, such as anticipating the things needed for a camping trip or for a visit to the beach (Atance 2008; Atance and Jackson 2009; Atance and Meltzoff 2005; Atance and O'Neill 2005; Fabricius 1988; Guajardo and Best 2000; Hudson, Shapiro, and Sosa 1995). In doing so, they become more skilled at mentally putting themselves into the future in order to anticipate what they will need and to plan in the present.

Of course, those skills apply to familiar events. When unfamiliar events are concerned—such as the first trip to the dentist—children rely entirely on the adult's description of a new experience in anticipating what it will be like. The adult's portrayal of that experience can influence young children's expectations of what will occur.

Young children's conversations with adults are important in helping the children anticipate and plan for future events. Adults are important for helping young children understand the time context in which future events will occur (e.g., "four sleeps" before a doctor's appointment; "after your birthday"; until next Halloween), as well as how to prepare for future events (Hudson 2002, 2006). Indeed, young children's concepts of time depend on how their understanding of future events is structured through conversations with family members who anticipate those events. It is important to remember again, however, that every family has its own cultural practices, and those unique practices may lead to different ways of recalling and anticipating events in time (Gauvain 2004). For example, in some cultures, children have been socialized to plan with an individual goal in mind; in other cultures, they plan a goal that is cooperatively shared. In addition, the everyday activities of children with their families and other caregivers contribute to children's understanding of time. These include the sequence of daily routines in which certain events follow other events (e.g., mealtime and then brushing teeth; story and then bedtime), explicit references to clocks and calendars, and behaviors that anticipate future events (e.g., getting out coats when the weather turns cold) (Benson 1997).

Personal History

A sense of time is also characterized by the awareness of one's own growth over time. For adults, this involves the recognition of how one's skills, knowledge, and experience change over time and how personal memories tell a life story. For an adult, these memories may consist of significant (e.g., graduating from school; first meeting a life partner) and ordinary experiences (e.g., an enjoyable baseball game with a family member) that are remembered because they are personally meaningful in some way. Autobiographical memories and the awareness of one's own development combine to create a sense of personal history.

Preschoolers are just at the beginning of creating a sense of personal history. For older three- and four-year-olds, a sense of personal history consists primarily of their pleasure in noticing the development of new skills and abilities. Their pride in these new accomplishments is reflected in their efforts to draw the attention of adults to their skills. The adult's acknowledgment of these abilities, perhaps with comments that the child could not do them a few months earlier, helps young children see how much they are learning and growing.

Older four- and five-year-olds are beginning to construct a more expanded sense of their own past in two ways. First, they often spontaneously compare their current abilities with those of the past, such as telling the teacher that they can now do things that they could not do when they were little (Harter 1999, 2006; Stipek and Mac Iver 1985). Their spontaneous comparison of current and past abilities contributes to older preschoolers' pride in their skills and positive self-esteem. Second, five-year-olds are also beginning to construct autobiographical memories of recent personal experiences. These memories

are different from other kinds of recollections because the child is the central figure in these events and remembers them because they are personally meaningful (Nelson and Fivush 2004). Thus, even though young children may share ordinary experiences—a trip to the supermarket, playing with a new pet—they are remembered and shared with adults because the child has found them meaningful.

Research on early autobiographical memory indicates, moreover, that the process of sharing these memories and discussing them with an adult is important to how these events are remembered (Farrant and Reese 2000; Hudson 1990; Nelson and Fivush 2004; Reese 2002). In their response to the child, adults ask questions that help to deepen and expand children's recollections of these events. They also help to organize the child's memory of what happened so the event becomes more easily remembered in the future. Adults also help children clarify their own feelings and reactions to these experiences in a manner that contributes to developing self-awareness. Therefore, when adults take the time to converse with young children about the experiences that children want to share, they contribute significantly to the growth of autobiographical memory and to the development of the child's sense of personal history.

Historical Changes in People and the World

Anyone who spends time with preschoolers is likely to be impressed with their interest in dinosaurs, knights, castles, pirates, kings and princesses, and other historical characters that have been highlighted in stories, commercial products, and the media. Young children enjoy learning about these events of "long ago," but their historical sense is limited by an inability to place these events appropriately within a broader historical timeline. Just as children have difficulty sequencing events of their own past in relation to each other (as noted above), they have even greater difficulty understanding how events in the past are sequenced on a longer **timeline** in relation to each other (Barton and Levstik 1996; Friedman 1992, 2003, 2005, 2007; Friedman and Kemp 1998; Levstik and Barton 1996).

By age four, children can distinguish events of the recent past (such as last Halloween) from events of "long ago" (such as when dinosaurs lived and pioneers explored the country), but they cannot place these events in any consistent historical sequence. Their confusion is increased by their exposure to commercial media (such as cartoons) that obscure historical understanding through fictional reconstructions.

By age five, children begin to understand that there is a sequence of historical events on a timeline and start to grasp where events occur on that timeline. In a sense, young children's sense of history is like an accordion. At first, every event that did not occur recently took place "long ago," and subsequently children make a distinction between the "long ago" of dinosaurs and when their grandparents were little children.

Later, as young children learn more about events of the past, the accordion expands as children better understand the historical timeline in which events occurred. Preschoolers are only at the beginning of this developmental process. It will be several years before children become capable of creating a mental historical timeline in which these events and others can be accurately placed.

Four-year-olds readily distinguish young from older people in their families and in the world at large. Older four- and five-year-olds also become interested in family history. They enjoy hearing stories of when their family members were children, and what the world was like when their grandparents were young, although their perception that these were also events that happened "long ago" can add to their confusion (e.g., did Grandpa live when the dinosaurs lived?). In contrast to four-year-olds, five-year-olds not only can distinguish younger and older people, but also have a stronger interest in and understanding of family history. They readily grasp the different ages of family members, understand that life was different when grandparents were children, and begin to comprehend the family history that has brought them to the present moment. Although adults can contribute to clarifying children's historical understanding, children work to comprehend when all these events occurred in relation to each other until middle childhood, when they begin to create their own mental timeline of events.

Sense of Place (Geography and Ecology)

Navigating Familiar Locations

The "sense of place" that emerges earliest for young children is their experience of familiar locations, such as their home, school, and the routes connecting them. For young children, familiar locations are limited to the home, extended family, and other care settings where children spend the most time. As children mature through the preschool years, their concept of place expands to encompass the broader communities in which they live: their neighborhood, city, or rural region in which they travel with their families. In each case, children's developing sense of place is reflected in their capacities to describe the characteristics of terrains with which they are familiar, and to describe the associations between locations and landmarks in these terrains. For a four-year-old, a home is where one finds a bed, dresser, and clothing and where one sleeps; a preschool setting is where one finds a dress-up area, reading area, and a place for circle time. For a five-year-old, this advancing understanding may be manifested in the acknowledgment that she lives in a community where many children play soccer, there is much rain, and people have to drive long distances to reach places.

At the same time, young children are developing a sense of relative location. Four-year-olds are beginning to use appropriate words to indicate directions in familiar locations, such as *over* or *in*, but are not always helpful to an uninitiated observer. Five-year-olds are beginning to indicate the relative distances between familiar locations in the home community—for example, a boy knowing that his grandmother's house is a long distance from home. However, because young children judge relative distances subjectively (e.g., how long is the ride in the car or bus to get to Grandma's house?), these general directional judgments may be misleading.

Caring for the Natural World

Young children enjoy the natural world and learning about it, and researchers and early educators have studied children's developing understanding of **natural phenomena** (e.g., Catling 2006; Kahn and Kellert 2002). Beyond confirming young children's strong interest in the natural world, research has highlighted several other points.

First, an appreciation of **ecology** and of human–environment interactions begins early. Young children enjoy providing nurturance to plants and animals and watching them grow, especially when teachers help them understand the connection between feeding and watering and the health and growth of a plant or a class pet. This experience can also contribute meaningfully to their sense of human growth and development. Young children also gain early awareness of the negative effects of human action on the environment (Cohen and Horm-Wingerd 1993; Musser and Diamond 1999). From an early age, young preschoolers are aware of the hazards of pollution, litter, and other forms of human harm, but it is primarily in the fifth year that they become capable of connecting their own actions (such as picking up litter and recycling) to the broader problems of environmental pollution and diminishing resources.

Second, understanding the natural world is also based on a young child's direct experiences. A young child growing up on a farm has much more direct experience with domestic and wild animals, open spaces, and thunderstorms than does a child living in urban Los Angeles. Given the importance of direct experience for a young preschooler's interest in and understanding of the natural world (and the need for early childhood educators to build on that natural curiosity), the ways in which young children learn about the natural world will vary depending on the ecological context in which each child lives. Many modern commentators (e.g., Luov 2005) worry about children growing up today in urban settings and who lack experience with the natural world.

Third, as children mature cognitively from ages three to five, their capacity to understand natural phenomena that are not part of their everyday experience expands (Gelman 2003). Opportunities for children to learn about the natural world significantly increases as children become interested in natural environments (e.g., the Arctic, tropical climates, or jungle settings) that are different from their own and in aspects of the biological world (from the microscopic to the cosmic) that they can experience only indirectly.

Finally, young children develop an **intuitive** understanding of the natural world that is sometimes consistent with adult understanding and sometimes surprisingly unique (Coley, Solomon, and Shafto 2002; Gelman 2003). For example, preschoolers have a remarkably accurate appreciation of biological inheritance—in other words, that offspring inevitably resemble their parents—and that babies grow up to be like their biological parents regardless of how or with whom they are raised. But preschoolers are uncertain about whether adopted children will most resemble their adoptive or biological parents. Preschoolers' inability to see the germs that cause infections also confuse them about whether germs are biological organisms or are

more like poisons. As these examples illustrate, a young child's remarkable awareness of aspects of the natural world can lead adults to overestimate the extent to which children's knowledge and reasoning is adultlike. Sometimes it can be more helpful to expand young children's understanding by first asking children about what they already know—or want to know—about the natural world.

Understanding the Physical World Through Drawings and Maps

Maps, globes, and other physical representations are important means by which young children can acquire geographical understanding without direct experience with the landscape. Considerable research has been devoted to understanding the development of children's map-reading abilities (Liben 2006; National Research Council 2006; Newcombe and Huttenlocher 2000). Not surprisingly, map-reading is a challenging skill, requiring that young children understand how a two-dimensional drawing corresponds to a three-dimensional landscape, how to interpret map symbols, and how to locate themselves and other objects according to the map. Even more challenging is learning how to use a map, understanding how map symbols correspond to the real world in order to facilitate problem solving (such as identifying how to go from one location to another). Surprisingly, by the age of three, children understand how maps refer to physical landscapes; by four, they can interpret common objects on the landscape, such as roads, rivers and lakes, and mountains. But interpretation of map symbols is a challenge because symbols commonly combine meaningful (e.g., a line to rep-

HISTORY-SOCIAL SCIENCE

resent a road) and arbitrary (e.g., the color of the line) aspects that may be confusing to young children (who may expect the road also to be red). It is not until middle childhood that children are capable of appropriate interpretation of map symbols.

Older preschoolers enjoy creating their own maps of familiar settings and are also more skilled at using maps to solve simple problems, such as locating a hidden object in a room on the basis of a map (Blades and Cooke 2001; Blaut and others 2003; Bluestein and Acredolo 1979). Solving simple problems with maps requires understanding not only how the map refers to an actual landscape, but also how distances on the small map translate in **scale** to larger distances in the landscape. Although there is some evidence that five-year-olds can accomplish this with very simple maps, this skill is not fully achieved until middle childhood (Liben 2002; Liben and Yekel 1996; Uttal 1996; Vasilyeva and Huttenlocher 2004). Likewise, the maps of familiar settings that children create, such as representations of their preschool program or homes, often show inaccurate distances between objects, suggesting that scaling is a common problem in each instance (Liben 2002). Even so, older preschoolers enjoy creating maps and models (such as on a sand table) of real and imagined landscapes as they exercise their representational skills in understanding the physical world.

Marketplace (Economics)

Exchange

In today's society, young children are economic **consumers** from an early age, primarily through their efforts to convince adults to purchase goods and services on their behalf that they desire (commercial advertising readily enlists young children to do so). To understand adult roles, relationships, and responsibilities, however, children need to go beyond the desire-based role of a consumer. Many studies have examined preschoolers' knowledge of economic concepts and reveal their limited understanding of **economic exchange** (Berti and Bombi 1981, 1988; Burris 1983; Jahoda 1979, 1981; Leiser 1983; Schug 1987; Schug and Birkey 1985; Siegler and Thompson 1998; Thompson and Siegler 2000.) Older three-year-olds take pleasure in playing store or barbershop, pretend activities in which money is exchanged for goods or services.

But children of this age have little understanding of why money functions in this way, regarding it as a social custom rather than as a means of economic exchange or a financial transaction based on value. Furthermore, children of this age are still developing understanding about the relative value of the coins with which they are familiar, commonly intuiting that nickels are of greater value than dimes because they are larger.

By contrast, older four-year-olds have a somewhat more sophisticated economic understanding. They are aware that **bartering** can sometimes substitute for a monetary exchange, such as when one person offers to exchange an apple for a friend's orange. When playing store, children in the role of cashiers can be observed making change for a customer. Children of this age are also aware of how pricing is associated with value. Prices are higher for multiple goods (three apples compared with one) and for

HISTORY–SOCIAL SCIENCE

goods and services of greater value. One study has also shown that five-year-olds are sensitive to how demand can affect sales (Siegler and Thompson 1998). They realize, for example, that children at a lemonade stand are likely to sell more drinks on a hot day than on a cold one. All of these emerging economic concepts reflect the primarily consumer-oriented economic thinking of a preschooler. The central focus is toward the individual who wants something and the economic transactions necessary to obtain it.

It is important to appreciate how much is lacking in this economic approach. During the primary grades, children begin to comprehend many economic concepts. In contrast, preschoolers have little or no appreciation, for example, of the influence of the profit motive on the part of a seller or that a merchant is interested in selling goods and services for more than their cost to him or her. Preschoolers are unaware of the influence of economic competition on prices or of how competition can enable buyers to obtain goods and services at lower prices. They are also unaware of how pricing is affected by high or low demand, high or low supply, or the economic well-being of buyers. Indeed, preschoolers' economic naiveté leaves them vulnerable to misunderstanding the nature of the market in which they are consumers. They are likely to believe, for example, that commercial advertisements function like public service announcements to ensure that consumers are aware of desirable products and that sellers perform a valuable public service by enabling buyers to obtain the goods and services they want. They are also likely to be unaware of how a buyer's (e.g., a family member) strategic shopping may yield a better price for a product (e.g., a toy) that the consumer (i.e., the child) wants immediately.

Glossary

autobiographical memory. Memory of personal events in one's life.

bartering. Trading by exchanging things of value rather than money.

civics. Study of the privileges and obligations of citizens.

consumer. A person who uses (and thus may purchase) something of value, such as an object or a service.

ecology. The field of biology concerned with the relationship between organisms (including humans) and the environment.

economic exchange. Giving one thing of value for another thing of value, such as giving money to a shopkeeper to purchase food.

in-group bias. The tendency of people to prefer the characteristics of their own group. In young children, this does not necessarily mean that they are negative toward other groups.

intuitive. Understanding something by one's own reasoning rather than by learning from another.

mental "scripts." Understanding of how things happen in familiar routines, such as what occurs when going to a restaurant, getting ready for bed, and so on.

moral standards. Expectations for behavior that are based on the needs and welfare of people, such as not harming another; they tend to be consistent in different situations.

narrative practices. Activities shared between people (such as a parent and child) involving the use of language to create a story or account, such as talking about a shared experience, storytelling, or reading a book.

natural phenomena. Things that can be observed in the natural world, such as plants and animals, the stars, sun and moon, insects, and other objects and events.

pro-social. Positive and cooperative; sharing with another child is an example of pro-social behavior.

scale. The proportional relationship of a unit on one area (such as a map) and how it corresponds to a unit in the real world that it represents. A map scale is necessary for reading a map because one must understand how distances on the map correspond to distances in the region that the map represents.

social conventional standards. Expectations for behavior that are based on maintaining social order, such as sitting in the right place for circle time; they may differ depending on the context.

timeline. The linear sequence of events in time. Children understand, for example, that grandparents were born before parents were, or that George Washington lived before Abraham Lincoln.

References and Source Materials

Aboud, F. E. 1984. "Social and Cognitive Bases of Ethnic Identity Constancy." *Journal of Genetic Psychology* 145:217–30.

———. 1987. "The Development of Ethnic Self-Identification and Attitudes." In *Children's Ethnic Socialization*, edited by J. S. Phinney and M. J. Rotheram, 32–55. Newbury Park, CA: Sage Publications.

———. 1988. *Children and Prejudice*. New York: Blackwell.

———. 2003. "The Formation of In-Group Favoritism and Out-Group Prejudice in Young Children: Are They Distinct Attitudes?" *Developmental Psychology* 39:48–60.

———. 2008. "A Social–Cognitive Developmental Theory of Prejudice." In *Handbook of Race, Racism, and the Developing Child*, edited by S. M. Quintana and C. McKown, 55–71. New York: Wiley.

Atance, C. M. 2008. "Future Thinking in Young Children." *Current Directions in Psychological Science* 17 (4): 295–98.

Atance, C. M., and L. K. Jackson. 2009. "The Development and Coherence of Future-Oriented Behaviors During the Preschool Years." *Journal of Experimental Child Psychology* 102 (4): 379–91.

Atance, C. M., and A. N. Meltzoff. 2005. "My Future Self: Young Children's Ability to Anticipate and Explain Future States." *Cognitive Development* 20 (3): 341–61.

Atance, C. M., and D. K. O'Neill. 2005. "The Emergence of Episodic Future Thinking in Humans." *Learning and Motivation* 36 (2): 126–44.

Aukrust, V. G., and C. E. Snow. 1998. "Narratives and Explanations During Mealtime Conversations in Norway and the U.S." *Language in Society* 27 (2): 221–46.

Banks, J. A. 2006. *Cultural Diversity and Education: Foundations, Curriculum, and Teaching*. 5th ed. Boston, MA: Pearson/Allyn and Bacon.

Barbarin, O. A., and E. Odom. 2009. "Promoting Social Acceptance and Respect for Cultural Diversity in Young Children: Learning from Developmental Research." In *Handbook of Child Development and Early Education: Research to Practice*, edited by O. A. Barbarin and B. H. Wasik, 247–65. New York: Guilford Press.

Barton, K. C., and L. S. Levstik. 1996. "Back When God Was Around and Everything: Elementary Children's Understanding of Historical Time." *American Educational Research Journal* 33:419–54.

Bennett, M., and F. Sani. 2008. "Children's Subjective Identification with Social Groups." In *Intergroup Attitudes and Relations in Childhood Through Adulthood*, edited by S. R. Levy and M. Killen, 19–31. Oxford, UK: Oxford University Press.

Benson, J. B. 1997. "The Development of Planning: It's About Time." In *The Developmental Psychology of Planning: Why, How, and When Do We Plan?*, edited by S. L. Friedman and E. K. Scholnick, 43–75. Mahwah, NJ: Erlbaum Publishers.

Berlin, L. J., J. Cassidy, and K. Appleyard. 2008. "The Influence of Early Attachments on Other Relationships." In *Handbook of Attachment: Theory, Research, and Clinical Applications*, 2nd ed., edited by J. Cassidy and P. R. Shaver, 333–47. New York: Guilford Press.

Berti, A. E., and A. S. Bombi. 1981. "The Development of the Concept of Money and Its Value: A Longitudinal Study." *Child Development* 52 (4): 1179–82.

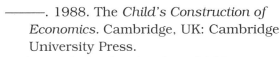

———. 1988. The *Child's Construction of Economics*. Cambridge, UK: Cambridge University Press.

Bigler, R. S., and L. S. Liben. 2007. "Developmental Intergroup Theory: Explaining and Reducing Children's Social Stereotyping and Prejudice." *Current Directions in Psychological Science* 16 (3): 162–66.

Birch, S., and G. Ladd. 1997. "The Teacher–Child Relationship and Children's Early School Adjustment." *Journal of School Psychology* 35 (1): 61–79.

Blades, M., and Z. Cooke. 2001. "Young Children's Ability to Understand a Model as a Spatial Representation." *Journal of Genetic Psychology* 155 (2): 201–18.

Blaut, J. M., and others. 2003. "Mapping as a Cultural and Cognitive Universal." *Annals of the Association of American Geographers* 93 (1): 165–85.

Bluestein, N., and L. Acredolo. 1979. "Developmental Changes in Map-Reading Skills." *Child Development* 50 (3): 691–97.

Bowman, B. T., M. S. Donovan, and M. S. Burns, eds. 2001. *Eager to Learn: Educating Our Preschoolers*. National Research Council and Committee on Early Childhood Pedagogy. Washington, DC: National Academies Press.

Bowman, B. T., and E. K. Moore. 2006. *School Readiness and Social Emotional Development: Perspectives on Cultural Diversity*. Washington, DC: National Black Child Development Institute.

Bronson, M. B. 2000. *Self-Regulation in Early Childhood: Nature and Nurture*. New York: Guilford Press.

Brown, C. S., and R. S. Bigler. 2005. "Children's Perceptions of Discrimination: A Developmental Model." *Child Development* 76 (3): 533–53.

Burris, V. 1983. "Stages in the Development of Economic Concepts." *Human Relations* 36 (9): 791–812.

Busby, J., and T. Suddendorf. 2005. "Recalling Yesterday and Predicting Tomorrow." *Cognitive Development* 20 (3): 362–72.

CDE (California Department of Education). 2005. *History–Social Science Content Standards for California Public Schools, Kindergarten Through Grade Twelve*. Sacramento: California Department of Education.

Calkins, S. D., and A. P. Williford. 2009. "Taming the Terrible Twos: Self-Regulation and School Readiness." In *Handbook of Child Development and Early Education: Research to Practice*, edited by O. A. Barbarin and B. H. Wasik, 172–98. New York: Guilford Press.

Carta, J. J., and others. 2000. *Project Slide: Skills for Learning Independence in Developmentally Appropriate Environments*. Longmont, CO: Sopris West Educational Services.

Catling, S. 2006. "What Do Five-Year-Olds Know of the World? Geographical Understanding and Play in Young Children's Early Learning." *Geography* 91 (2): 55–74.

Cohen, S., and D. Horm-Wingerd. 1993. "Children and the Environment: Ecological Awareness Among Preschool Children." *Environment and Behavior* 25 (1): 103–20.

Coley, J. D., G. E. A. Solomon, and P. Shafto. 2002. "The Development of Folkbiology: A Cognitive Science Perspective on Children's Understanding of the Biological World." In *Children and Nature: Psychological, Sociocultural, and Evolutionary Investigation*, edited by P. Kahn and S. Kellert, 65–91. Cambridge, MA: MIT Press.

Denham, S. 1998. *Emotional Development in Young Children*. New York: Guilford Press.

———. 2006. "The Emotional Basis of Learning and Development in Early Childhood Education." In *Handbook of Research on the Education of Young Children,* 2nd ed., edited by B. Spodek and O. N. Saracho, 85–103. Mahwah, NJ: Erlbaum.

Dunn, J. 1993. *Young Children's Close Relationships: Beyond Attachment.* Newbury Park, CA: Sage Publications.

Edwards, C. P., and others. 2006. "Parental Ethnotheories of Child Development: Looking Beyond Independence and Individualism in American Belief Systems." In *Indigenous and Cultural Psychology: Understanding People in Context,* edited by U. Kim, K. S. Yang, and K. K. Hwang, 141–62. New York: Springer Publishing Company.

Edwards, C. P., and P. G. Ramsey. 1986. *Promoting Social and Moral Development in Young Children: Creative Approaches for the Classroom.* New York: Teachers College Press.

Fabes, R. A., and N. Eisenberg. 1992. "Young Children's Coping with Interpersonal Anger." *Child Development* 63 (1): 116–28.

Fabricius, W. 1988. "The Development of Forward Search Planning in Preschoolers." *Child Development* 59 (6): 1473–88.

Farrant, K., and E. Reese. 2000. "Maternal Style and Children's Participation in Reminiscing: Stepping Stones in Children's Autobiographical Memory Development." *Journal of Cognition and Development* 1 (2): 193–225.

Fivush, R. 2001. "Owning Experience: Developing Subjective Perspective in Autobiographical Narratives." In *The Self in Time,* edited by C. Moore and K. Lemmon, 35–52. Mahwah, NJ: Erlbaum.

Friedman, W. J. 1991. "The Development of Children's Memory for the Time of Past Events." *Child Development* 62 (1): 139–55.

———. 1992. "Children's Time Memory: The Development of a Differentiated Past." *Cognitive Development* 7 (2): 171–87.

———. 2000. "The Development of Children's Knowledge of the Times of Future Events." *Child Development* 71 (4): 913–32.

———. 2002. "Children's Knowledge of the Future Distances of Daily Activities and Annual Events." *Journal of Cognition and Development* 3 (3): 333–56.

———. 2003. "The Development of a Differentiated Sense of the Past and the Future." In Vol. 31 of *Advances in Child Development and Behavior,* edited by R. V. Kail, 229–69. San Diego, CA: Academic (Elsevier).

———. 2005. "Developmental and Cognitive Perspectives on Humans' Sense of the Times of Past and Future Events." *Learning and Motivation* 36 (2): 145–58.

———. 2007. "The Development of Temporal Metamemory." *Child Development* 78: 1472–91.

Friedman, W. J., A. G. Gardner, and N. R. E. Zubin. 1995. "Children's Comparisons of the Recency of Two Events from the Past Year." *Child Development* 66 (4): 970–83.

Friedman, W. J., and S. Kemp. 1998. "The Effects of Elapsed Time and Retrieval on Young Children's Judgments of the Temporal Distances of Past Events." *Cognitive Development* 13 (3): 335–67.

Gauvain, M. 2004. "Bringing Culture Into Relief: Cultural Contributions to the Development of Children's Planning Skills." In Vol. 32 of *Advances in Child Development and Behavior,* edited by R. V. Kail, 37–71. Amsterdam: Elsevier.

Gelman, S. A. 2003. *The Essential Child.* Oxford, UK: Oxford University Press.

Guajardo, N. R., and D. L. Best. 2000. "Do Preschoolers Remember What to Do? Incentive and External Cues in Prospective Memory." *Cognitive Development* 15:75–97.

Hamre, B. K., and R. C. Pianta. 2001. "Early Teacher–Child Relationships and the Trajectory of Children's School Outcomes Through Eighth Grade." *Child Development* 72 (2): 625–38.

HISTORY–SOCIAL SCIENCE

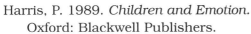

Harris, P. 1989. *Children and Emotion.* Oxford: Blackwell Publishers.

———. 2006. "Social Cognition." In Vol. 2 of *Handbook of Child Psychology: Cognition, Perception and Language,* 6th ed., edited by W. Damon, R. M. Lerner, D. Kuhn, and R. Siegler (vol. eds.), 811–58. New York: Wiley.

Harter, S. 1999. *The Construction of the Self: A Developmental Perspective.* New York: Guilford Press.

———. 2006. "The Self." In Vol. 3 of *Handbook of Child Psychology: Social, Emotional, and Personality Development,* 6th ed., edited by W. Damon and R. M. Lerner (series eds.), 505–70. New York: Wiley.

Hartup, W. W. 1996. "The Company They Keep: Friendships and Their Developmental Significance." *Child Development* 67 (1): 1–13.

Hirschfeld, L. A. 1996. *Race in the Making: Cognition, Culture, and the Child's Construction of Human Kinds.* Cambridge: MIT Press.

———. 2008. "Children's Developing Conceptions of Race." In *Handbook of Race, Racism, and the Developing Child,* edited by S. M. Quintana and C. McKown, 37–54. Hoboken, NJ: Wiley.

Howes, C. 1987. "Social Competence with Peers in Young Children: Developmental Sequences." *Developmental Review* 7 (3): 252–72.

———. 1988. "Peer Interaction of Young Children." *Monographs of the Society for Research in Child Development* 53 (1) (Serial no. 217).

———. 1992. *The Collaborative Construction of Pretend.* Albany: State University of New York Press.

Howes, C., and S. Spieker. 2008. "Attachment Relationships in the Context of Multiple Caregivers." In *Handbook of Attachment: Theory, Research, and Clinical Applications,* 2nd ed., edited by J. Cassidy and P. R. Shaver, 317–32. New York: Guilford Press.

Hudson, J. A. 1990. "The Emergence of Autobiographic Memory in Mother-Child Conversation." In *Knowing and Remembering in Young Children,* edited by R. Fivush and J. A. Hudson, 166–96. New York: Cambridge University Press.

———. 2002. "'Do You Know What We're Going to Do This Summer?' Mothers' Talk to Preschool Children about Future Events." *Journal of Cognition and Development* 3 (1): 49–71.

———. 2006. "The Development of Future Time Concepts Through Mother-Child Conversation." *Merrill-Palmer Quarterly* 52 1:70–95.

Hudson, J. A., L. R. Shapiro, and B. B. Sosa. 1995. "Planning in the Real World: Preschool Children's Scripts and Plans for Familiar Events." *Child Development* 66:984–98.

Jahoda, G. 1979. "The Construction of Economic Reality by Some Glaswegian Children." *European Journal of Social Psychology* 9:115–27.

———. 1981. "The Development of Thinking about Economic Institutions: The Bank." *Cahiers de Psychologie Cognitive* 1 (1): 55–73.

Kahn, P., and S. Kellert, eds. 2002. *Children and Nature: Psychological, Sociocultural, and Evolutionary Investigations.* Cambridge, MA: MIT Press.

Katz, P. A. 2003. "Racists or Tolerant Multiculturalists? How Do They Begin?" *American Psychologist* 58 (11): 807–909.

Kochanska, G., and R. A. Thompson. 1997. "The Emergence and Development of Conscience in Toddlerhood and Early Childhood." In *Parenting and Children's Internalization of Values,* edited by J. Grusec and L. Kuczynski, 53–77. New York: Wiley.

La Paro, K. M., and R. C. Pianta. 2000. "Predicting Children's Competence in the Early School Years: A Meta-Analytic Review." *Review of Educational Research* 70 (4): 443–84.

HISTORY–SOCIAL SCIENCE

Ladd, G. W., S. H. Birch, and E. S. Buhs. 1999. "Children's Social and Scholastic Lives in Kindergarten: Related Spheres of Influence?" *Child Development* 70 (6): 1373–1400.

Ladd, G. W., B. J. Kocherderfer, and C. C. Coleman. 1996. "Friendship Quality as a Predictor of Young Children's Early School Adjustment." *Child Development* 67 (3): 1103–18.

———. 1997. "Classroom Peer Acceptance, Friendship, and Victimization: Distinct Relational Systems That Contribute Uniquely to Children's School Adjustment?" *Child Development* 68 (6): 1181–97.

Laible, D. J., and R. A. Thompson. 2000. "Mother–Child Discourse, Attachment Security, Shared Positive Affect, and Early Conscience Development." *Child Development* 71 (5): 1424–40.

———. 2002. "Mother–Child Conflict in the Toddler Years: Lessons in Emotion, Morality, and Relationships." *Child Development* 73 (4): 1187–1203.

Lamb, M. E. 1998. "Nonparental Child Care: Context, Quality, Correlates." In Vol. 4 of *Handbook of Child Psychology: Child Psychology in Practice*, 5th ed., edited by W. Damon. I. E. Sigel and K. A. Renninger (vol. eds.), 73–134. New York: Wiley.

Leiser, D. 1983. "Children's Conceptions of Economics: The Constitution of a Cognitive Domain." *Journal of Economic Psychology* 4 (4): 297–317.

Levstik, L. S., and K. C. Barton. 1996. "'They Still Use Some of Their Past: Historical Salience in Elementary Children's Chronological Thinking." *Journal of Curriculum Studies* 28:531–76.

Leyva, D., and others. 2008. "Elaboration and Autonomy Support in Low-Income Mothers' Reminiscing: Links to Children's Autobiographical Narratives." *Journal of Cognition and Development* 9 (4): 363–89.

Liben, L. S. 2002. "Spatial Development in Childhood: Where Are We Now?" In *Blackwell Handbook of Childhood Cognitive Development*, edited by U. Goswami, 326–48. Oxford, UK: Blackwell Publishers.

———. 2006. "Education for Spatial Thinking." In Vol. 4 of *Handbook of Child Psychology: Child Psychology in Practice*, 6th ed., W. Damon and R. M. Lerner (series eds.), K. A. Renninger and I. E. Sigel (vol. eds.), 197–247. New York: Wiley.

Liben, L. S., and C. A. Yekel. 1996. "Preschoolers' Understanding of Plan and Oblique Maps: The Role of Geometric and Representational Correspondence." *Child Development* 67 (6): 2780–96.

Luov, R. 2005. *Last Child in the Woods: Saving Our Children from Nature-Deficit Disorder.* Chapel Hill, NC: Algonquin Books.

Melzi, G., and M. Caspe. 2005. "Variations in Maternal Narrative Styles During Book Reading Interactions." *Narrative Inquiry* 15 (1): 101–25.

Mindes, G. 2005. "Social Studies in Today's Early Childhood Curricula." *Beyond the Journal: Young Children on the Web* 60 (5): 12–18.

Musser, L. M., and K. E. Diamond. 1999. "The Children's Attitudes Toward the Environment Scale for Preschool Children." *Journal of Environmental Education* 30 (2): 23–30.

National Research Council. 2006. *Learning to Think Spatially: GIS as a Support System in the K–12 Curriculum.* Washington, DC: National Academies Press.

Nelson, K. 2001. "Language and the Self: From the 'Experiencing I' to the 'Continuing Me.'" In *The Self in Time*, edited by C. Moore and K. Lemmon, 15–33. Mahwah, NJ: Erlbaum.

Nelson, K., and R. Fivush. 2004. "The Emergence of Autobiographical Memory: A Social-Cultural Developmental Theory." *Psychological Review* 111 (2): 486–511.

HISTORY–SOCIAL SCIENCE

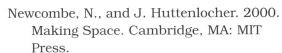

Newcombe, N., and J. Huttenlocher. 2000. *Making Space.* Cambridge, MA: MIT Press.

Parker, J. G., and J. M. Gottman. 1989. "Social and Emotional Development in a Relational Context: Friendship Interaction from Early Childhood to Adolescence." In *Peer Relations in Child Development,* edited by T. J. Berndt and G. W. Ladd, 95–132. New York: Wiley.

Peisner-Feinberg, E. S., and others. 2001. "The Relation of Preschool Child-Care Quality to Children's Cognitive and Social Developmental Trajectories Through Second Grade." *Child Development* 72 (5): 1534–53.

Perez-Granados, D. R., and M. A. Callanan. 1997. "Parents and Siblings as Early Resources for Young Children's Learning in Mexican-Descent Families." *Hispanic Journal of Behavioral Sciences* 19 (1): 3–33.

Pianta, R. C., S. L. Nimetz, and E. Bennett. 1997. "Mother–Child Relationships, Teacher–Child Relationships, and School Outcomes in Preschool and Kindergarten." *Early Childhood Research Quarterly* 12 (3): 263–80.

Pianta, R. C., M. S. Steinberg, and K. B. Rollins. 1995. "The First Two Years of School: Teacher–Child Relationships and Deflections in Children's Classroom Adjustment." *Development and Psychopathology* 7:295–312.

Pianta, R. C., and M. W. Stuhlman, 2004a. "Teacher–Child Relationships and Children's Success in the First Years of School." *School Psychology Review* 33 (3): 444–58.

———. 2004b. "Conceptualizing Risk in Relational Terms: Associations Among the Quality of Child–Adult Relationships Prior to School Entry and Children's Developmental Outcomes in First Grade." *Educational and Child Psychology* 21:32–45.

Povinelli, D. 1995. "The Unduplicated Self." In *The Self in Early Infancy,* edited by P. Rochat, 161–92. Amsterdam: North Holland-Elsevier.

———. 2001. "The Self: Elevated in Consciousness and Extended in Time." In *The Self in Time,* edited by C. Moore and K. Lemmon, 75–95. Mahwah, NJ: Erlbaum.

Povinelli, D., K. Landau, and H. Perilloux. 1996. "Self-Recognition in Young Children Using Delayed Versus Live Feedback: Evidence of a Developmental Asynchrony." *Child Development* 67: 1540–54.

Povinelli, D., and others. 1999. "Development of Young Children's Understanding That the Recent Past Is Causally Bound to the Present." *Developmental Psychology* 35 (6):1426–39.

Povinelli, D, and B. Simon. 1998. "Young Children's Understanding of Briefly Versus Extremely Delayed Images of the Self: Emergence of the Autobiographical Stance." *Developmental Psychology* 34:188–94.

Quintana, S. M. 1998. "Children's Developmental Understanding of Ethnicity and Race." *Applied and Preventive Psychology* 7 (1): 27–45.

———. 2007. "Racial and Ethnic Identity: Developmental Perspectives and Research." *Journal of Counseling Psychology* 54 (3): 259–270.

———. 2008. "Racial Perspective Taking Ability: Developmental, Theoretical, and Empirical Trends." In *Handbook of Race, Racism, and the Developing Child,* edited by S. M. Quintana and C. McKown, 16–36. New York: Wiley.

Reese, E. 2002. "Social Factors in the Development of Autobiographical Memory: The State of the Art." *Social Development* 11 (1): 124–42.

Rogoff, B. 1989. *Apprenticeship in Thinking: Cognitive Development in Social Context.* New York: Oxford University Press.

Rubin, K. H., W. M. Bukowski, and J. G. Parker. 2006. "Peer Interactions, Relationships, and Groups." In Vol. 3 of

HISTORY–SOCIAL SCIENCE

Handbook of Child Psychology: Social, Emotional, and Personality Development, 6th ed., edited by W. Damon and R. M. Lerner, 571–645. New York: Wiley.

Rubin, K. H., and others. 2005. "Peer Relationships in Childhood." In *Developmental Science: An Advanced Textbook*, 5th ed., edited by M. H. Bornstein and M. E. Lamb, 469–512. Mahwah, NJ: Erlbaum.

Schug, M. C. 1987. "Children's Understanding of Economics." *The Elementary School Journal* 87 (5): 506–18.

Schug, M. C., and J. C. Birkey 1985. "The Development of Children's Economic Reasoning." *Theory and Research in Social Education* 13 (1): 31–42.

Shonkoff, J. P., and D. A. Phillips, eds. 2000. *From Neurons to Neighborhoods: The Science of Early Childhood Development*. National Research Council and Institute of Medicine, Committee on Integrating the Science of Early Childhood Development. Washington, DC: National Academies Press.

Siegler, R. S., and D. R. Thompson. 1998. "'Hey, Would You Like a Nice Cold Cup of Lemonade On This Hot Day?' Children's Understanding of Economic Causation." *Developmental Psychology* 34 (1): 146–60.

Smetana, J. G. 1981. "Preschool Children's Conceptions of Moral and Social Rules." *Child Development* 52 (4): 1333–36.

———. 1985. "Preschool Children's Conceptions of Transgressions: The Effects of Varying Moral and Conventional Domain-Related Attributes." *Developmental Psychology* 21 (1): 18–29.

Smetana, J. G., and J. L. Braeges. 1990. "The Development of Toddler's Moral and Conventional Judgments." *Merrill-Palmer Quarterly* 36 (3): 329–46.

Stipek, D., and D. Mac Iver. 1985. "Developmental Change in Children's Assessment of Intellectual Competence." *Child Development* 60:521–38.

Thompson, D. R., and R. S. Siegler. 2000. "Buy Low, Sell High: The Development of an Informal Theory of Economics." *Child Development* 71 (3): 660–77.

Thompson, J. E., and K. K. Twibell. 2009. "Teaching Hearts and Minds in Early Childhood Classrooms: Curriculum for Social and Emotional Development." In *Handbook of Child Development and Early Education: Research to Practice*, edited by O. A. Barbarin and B. H. Wasik, 199–222. New York: Guilford Press.

Thompson, R. A. 1990. "Emotion and Self-Regulation." In Vol. 36 of *Socioemotional Development* (Nebraska Symposium on Motivation), edited by R. A. Thompson, 383–483. Lincoln, NE: University of Nebraska Press.

———. 1994. "Emotion Regulation: A Theme in Search of Definition." In *The Development of Emotion Regulation and Dysregulation: Biological and Behavioral Aspects*, edited by N. A. Fox. Monographs of the Society for Research in *Child Development* 59 (2–3): 25–52 (Serial no. 240).

———. 1998. "Empathy and Its Origins in Early Development." In *Intersubjective Communication and Emotion in Early Ontogeny: A Source Book*, edited by S. Braten, 144–57. New York: Cambridge University Press.

———. 2002. "The Roots of School Readiness in Social and Emotional Development." *The Kauffman Early Education Exchange* 1:8–29.

———. 2006. "The Development of the Person: Social Understanding, Relationships, Self, Conscience." In Vol. 3 of *Handbook of Child Psychology: Social, Emotional, and Personality Development*, 6th ed., edited by W. Damon and R. M. Lerner. N. Eisenberg (vol. eds.), 24–98. New York: Wiley.

Thompson, R. A., and M. Goodman. 2009. "Development of Self, Relationships, and Socioemotional Competence: Foundations for Early School Success."

In *Handbook of Child Development and Early Education: Research to Practice*, edited by O. A. Barbarin and B. H. Wasik, 147–71. New York: Guilford Press.

Thompson, R. A., R. Goodvin, and S. Meyer. 2006. "Social Development: Psychological Understanding, Self-Understanding, and Relationships." In *Handbook of Preschool Mental Health: Development, Disorders, and Treatment,* edited by J. Luby, 3–22. New York: Guilford Press.

Thompson, R. A., and K. Lagattutta. 2006. "Feeling and Understanding: Early Emotional Development." In *The Blackwell Handbook of Early Childhood Development,* edited by K. McCartney and D. Phillips, 317–37. Oxford, UK: Blackwell Publishers.

Thompson, R. A., S. Meyer, and M. McGinley. 2006. "Understanding Values in Relationship: The Development of Conscience." In *Handbook of Moral Development,* edited by M. Killen and J. Smetana, 267–97. Mahwah, NJ: Erlbaum.

Thompson, R. A., and H. A. Raikes. 2007. "The Social and Emotional Foundations of School Readiness." In *Social and Emotional Health in Early Childhood: Building Bridges Between Services and Systems,* edited by D. F. Perry, R. F. Kaufmann, and J. Knitzer, 13–35. Baltimore, MD: Paul H. Brookes Publishing Co.

Thompson, R. A., and J. E. Thompson. 2010. "Early Childhood Education for Children with Disabilities." *The Special EDge* 23:1–6.

Uttal, D. H. 1996. "Angles and Distances: Children's and Adults' Reconstruction and Scaling of Spatial Configurations." *Child Development* 67 (6): 2763–79.

Vasilyeva, M., and J. Huttenlocher. 2004. "Early Development of Scaling Ability." *Developmental Psychology* 40 (5): 682–90.

Early childhood education standards from the following states were examined in the preparation of these foundations: Florida, Georgia, Hawaii, Illinois, Kentucky, Massachusetts, Michigan, Texas, and Washington.

HISTORY–SOCIAL SCIENCE

FOUNDATIONS IN
Science

The study of science is about finding out how the world works. Young children, like scientists, have a sense of wonder and natural curiosity about objects and events in their environment. From infancy, they actively engage in making sense of their world. They build with blocks, move toy cars in different ways, collect rocks, and play with dirt, water, and sand. Children's play and exploration have much in common with the scientific processes employed by scientists. Through exploration and experimentation with objects and materials in their home or preschool environment, children learn the properties of objects: size, weight, shape, what they are made of, their function, and how they move. They discover what different animals and plants look like and how they live, grow, and change over time. Everyday experiences provide children with many opportunities to ask questions, to make sense of what they observe, and to build a coherent understanding of the world around them.

Developmental research indicates that the majority of children are ready to learn and reason about many of the scientific concepts that naturally capture their interest. From infancy, they actively construct fundamental concepts of the physical and biological world. Throughout the preschool period, children develop scientific concepts and gain knowledge about objects and events in their everyday environment. By the time they enter school, they have a rich body of expectations and coherent sets of concepts about **living things** and physical objects (Spelke 1990; Baillargeon 1995; Gelman 2003; Inagaki and Hatano 2002; Bullock, Gelman, and Baillargeon 1982).

Children's **predisposition** to learn certain kinds of knowledge, and to think abstractly about concepts from biology and physics, support the early learning of science and pave the way for competence in early schooling. Children's natural inclination and ability to observe and try to understand their world, to develop conceptual knowledge, and to reason about many scientific concepts make science an excellent fit for the preschool environment. As such, there is growing recognition at the national level that science is appropriate and important for preschool children (National Research Council 1999, 2000, 2007).

Science in Preschool

Science in preschool is built on children's natural curiosity and tendency to actively explore, experiment, and discover the nature of things in their everyday life. It is not about a discrete body of knowledge or a list of facts presented to children. This approach to preschool science is consistent with a **constructivist approach** on learning, in which children construct knowledge and build theories by interacting with the environment rather than passively taking in information (Chaille and Britain 2002). Science in the preschool years is about children observing and investigating objects and events in their environment. Through a planned, play-based, supportive environment, they expand their existing knowledge and experience of their everyday world. Science is about providing children with the basic skills of **scientific inquiry**, such as observing and describing, **comparing and contrasting**, classifying, experimenting and **recording**, and using the scientific vocabulary associated with these skills. Science in the preschool years not only prepares children for the scientific skills and knowledge they will encounter in school, but also supports their development in different domains, including social–emotional development, language and literacy, and mathematics.

Development of the Whole Child (Science and Other Domains)

Science in preschool fosters a joy of discovery and a positive approach to learning. Making discoveries, identifying solutions, and trying to figure things out develops children's initiative in learning and helps them become self-confident learners. Science fosters skills that are recognized as critical for success in work and in life in the twenty-first century: critical thinking, problem solving, creativity, collaboration, and **communication** (Bellanca and Brandt 2010). In scientific investigation, children become learners who ask questions, solve problems, propose new ways of doing things, and make decisions based on reasoning. Science experiences also develop children's ability to interact with peers and adults, share ideas, listen to others, and work cooperatively as competent group members—skills that are important to many areas of learning throughout life.

Early science experiences provide authentic situations to learn and use language and literacy skills. Science activities are typically hands-on, providing multiple ways for young children to make meaning of social and verbal interactions and to build language skills, vocabulary, and grammar. Scientific exploration exposes young children to a variety of new words in meaningful contexts, resulting in vocabulary gains (Brenneman, Stevenson-Boyd, and Frede 2009; French 2004). Although science is important for all children, it is especially relevant to English learners and many children with special needs, for whom the development of new vocabulary and language skills in authentic learning experiences is most effective. Conversations associated with scientific inquiry tend to be rich in language. Children develop both their comprehension and expressive language skills as they make predictions ("What will happen if?"), plan explorations, describe findings, and explain their reasoning (e.g., "Why did it happen?"). They reason and talk about future events and about past experiences. They also learn how to maintain a coherent conversation, listen to others, and stay on topic (Conezio and French 2002). Science provides many opportunities for a variety of preliteracy and literacy experiences. Fiction and nonfiction books about key science content ideas serve as a basis for conversations with adults and peers. Books also provide children with excellent opportunities for building vocabulary. Books with science content build on children's natural curiosity to explore and learn and foster an appreciation and enjoyment of reading. **Documentation** and recording of information on charts, graphs, books, and science journals also illustrates for children the link between spoken and written language and supports the development of print concepts.

Scientific inquiry experiences also provide children with opportunities to practice mathematical skills in a meaningful way and to use math as a tool for discovery. Fundamental mathematics concepts such as comparing, classifying, and measuring are important skills in scientific investigations (Lind 1997). The natural integration of mathematics and science begins in preschool. Consider, for example, the experience of observing and exploring the characteristics of a variety of pumpkins. Children may investigate and describe the pumpkins' sizes, weight, colors, shapes, and textures. They may **classify** the pumpkins by attributes; count the number in each category of pumpkins; compare the circumferences of two pumpkins by using a piece of yarn or a measuring tape (with adults' assistance); compare and contrast the inside and the out-

side of a pumpkin; order pumpkins by size from smallest to largest; estimate how many seeds are inside a pumpkin; and try to count to find the number of seeds. Such processes of observing and exploring pumpkins involve fundamental mathematical concepts such as number, shape, size, volume, and weight and the application of different mathematical skills, including counting, estimating, comparing, ordering, measuring, and classifying. (More about these mathematical skills can be found in the *California Preschool Learning Foundations, Volume 1* [CDE 2008].)

The Preschool Foundations for Science

The following section presents the California preschool learning foundations for the domain of science. The preschool science foundations are organized in four strands: Scientific Inquiry, Physical Sciences, Life Sciences, and Earth Sciences. The organization of the science foundations is aligned with the *Science Content Standards for California Public Schools* (Kindergarten) and the *National Science Education Content Standards* (National Committee on Science Education Standards and Assessment and National Research Council 1996). The first strand, Scientific Inquiry, is about basic language and skills that are fundamental to the process of doing science. The other three strands focus on scientific content: developmentally appropriate core ideas and concepts in the areas of **physical sciences**, **life sciences**, and **earth sciences**. Within each strand, the foundations describe the knowledge and skills most children who are typically developing demonstrate at around 48 and 60 months of age. The foundations are designed with the assumption that scientific knowledge and skills are developed through everyday interactions, activities, and play that are part of a supportive preschool environment. The foundations are illustrated by examples that put the scientific skill or knowledge into context. The examples illustrate the manifestation of a scientific competency through the behavior and reasoning of a particular child or children. As depicted by the examples, children at around 60 months of age typically demonstrate an increased ability in scientific skills and understanding compared with children of around 48 months of age. This increased ability at around 60 months as compared with the level at around 48 months may be manifested in a variety of ways, including a more sophisticated understanding of some scientific concepts, more frequent and more independent display of scientific inquiry, and an ability to describe **observations** in greater detail.

Individual, Cultural, and Linguistic Variations

As stated in the *National Science Education Content Standards,* "Science is for all students, regardless of age, sex, cultural ethnic background, disabilities, aspirations, or interest and motivation in science" (National Committee on Science Education Standards and Assessment and National Research Council 1996, 20). The goal in developing the preschool foundations for science is to describe age-appropriate scientific skills and knowledge that are typically displayed by preschool children under conditions that support healthy development. The foundations are meant to give teachers a general idea of what can be expected from children at around 48 and 60 months of age. The examples are meant to illustrate the different ways children may display their competencies; they are not assessment items of age-appropriate development. Children are different from one another and vary in their abilities, family and socioeconomic background, home experiences, and cultural heritage and values. Therefore, they may vary in the way they develop and display the knowledge and skills described in these foundations.

Children of comparable ages enter preschool with various linguistic, social, and cognitive skills. Some children may exhibit competencies that go beyond the level described in a particular foundation, while others may need more time to reach that level. The amount and kind of support they need varies from child to child. The application of these foundations requires the teacher's attention to the individual characteristics of the child. Children with disabilities or other special needs may require adaptations and various means of engagement and expression of scientific knowledge suited to their disability.

Children vary in their cultural backgrounds. As much as the development of scientific concepts is universal and salient in all cultures, cultural background may shape the development of some scientific concepts. Research indicates that the language to which children are exposed and culturally shared belief systems may play a role in children's development of core biological concepts and reasoning

(Anggoro, Waxman, and Medin 2005; Waxman and Medin 2006; Hatano and others 1993). Some cultures, for example, hold to a spiritual connection with nature, believing that humans are to live in harmony with nature rather than be in control of it. (See the Bibliographic Notes for more examples.) Understanding of biological concepts is also mediated by children's everyday experiences with the natural world. There are differences between urban children and rural children in the same society (Waxman, Medin, and Ross 2007). Even a simple activity, such as caring for a goldfish, can enhance aspects of urban children's biological thought (Inagaki 1990). It is important that teachers be sensitive to and respectful of the cultural backgrounds, home languages, family values, and everyday practices of the children in their groups in the application of the science foundations. Teachers should consider the different perspectives held by children, based on children's previous knowledge and experiences, and build on them to provide effective scientific experiences.

Children in California are diverse in terms of the languages they speak, and many are English learners. They learn about scientific concepts and skills while acquiring English. The science foundations emphasize the role of language and often rely on children's verbal abilities to describe their observations, make comparisons, **record** information, and share findings and explanations. However, children may also communicate their knowledge and skills nonverbally—through gestures, facial expressions, and actions. Many children who are English learners, for example, pass through a period of observation and listening before they

begin to express themselves in English. They still acquire knowledge and understanding of scientific concepts during this phase and may display their understanding nonverbally or in their home language.

Similarly, some children with special needs (e.g., children with speech or language delay) may express themselves by using nonverbal means of communication, through gestures, drawings, and actions. Teachers should be aware that when foundations or examples indicate verbal expression, children might use any means of communication (including home language, Sign Language, and communication devices) to display their knowledge. Having an adult to encourage, prompt, and scaffold the use of expressive language, in English and in the child's home language whenever possible, would support the child's overall development of scientific knowledge. For further information about English learners, consult the "Foundations in English-Language Development" in Volume 1 of the *California Preschool Learning Foundations* (CDE 2008).

Scientific Inquiry: The Skills and Language of Science

A fundamental assumption that guided the development of the preschool foundations for science is that children should learn about the content of science through active inquiry. Several national organizations, including the American Association for the Advancement of Science (1993) and the National Research Council (2007), have reached a consensus about the importance of offering to children experiences of scientific inquiry, developing investigation skills, and stimulating an interest in science (Lind 1999; Martin 2001). In experiences of scientific inquiry, children actively explore and develop knowledge and understanding of scientific ideas. They make observations, ask questions, plan **investigations**, gather and interpret information, propose explanations, and communicate findings and ideas. Although young children have a natural tendency to explore their environment, the processes and language of scientific inquiry allow them to explore objects and events in a systematic way. The first strand in the preschool science foundations, Scientific Inquiry, focuses on the skills and language employed in the process of scientific explorations.

The first substrand, Observation and Investigation, focuses on children's ability to observe and investigate objects and events in their everyday environment. Scientific investigations in the early years are largely based on systematic observations. Children use all their senses to gather information, and to construct meaning and knowledge. To expand their observation, they may also use scientific tools such as **measurement** or **observation tools**, with the guidance of adults in their environment. For example, when observing a leaf, they may use a magnifying glass to observe the "lines" more clearly or use a ruler (or unit blocks) to measure its length. Through observation, children begin to recognize and describe similarities and differences between one object and another. This is when they can start to compare and contrast objects and events and classify them based on different attributes. For example, a child might separate all the "pointy" leaves from all the round leaves or separate the big leaves from the small ones.

Children may also investigate objects and events by trying things to see what happens. For instance, they may investigate what happens to the toy car when it rolls down ramps with bumpy or smooth surfaces, test what happens to plants placed in locations with or without light, or test out their ideas of how to use pipes to make water go up and down in the water table. They learn to make **predictions** about changes in materials and objects based on their intuitive knowledge or past experience, and to test their predictions through observations or simple experiments. They can also make inferences and draw conclusions based on observable evidence, or based on their knowledge of objects and events, such as knowledge about categories of objects or the cause-and-effect relationships in events. The foundations in the first substrand include children's ability to ask questions, observe and describe observations, use scientific tools, compare and contrast, predict, and make inferences.

Communicating: The Role of Language in Scientific Inquiry

The second substrand under Scientific Inquiry, Documentation and Communication, is about processes and skills employed to document and record observations and to communicate ideas and explanations to others. Integral to the development of scientific inquiry skills is children's ability to use language and specific terms to describe their observations, plan explorations, and communicate findings, explanations, and ideas to others. Language allows children to become aware of their thoughts and to express them

54

in words (oral, written, or signed). Children who are English learners may have an understanding of the scientific concepts being explored, but they have not yet acquired the English vocabulary to describe their observations and express their thoughts. Observation and investigation experiences provide ideal opportunities to expose all children, including English learners, to new words and scientific vocabulary in English and in their home language, whenever possible.

Children learn new content words in meaningful contexts (Conezio and French 2002). They readily acquire vocabulary, such as new nouns, to describe what they are observing (e.g., *seeds, fins, nest, worms*), and adjectives to describe and compare the properties and characteristics of objects (e.g., *transparent, heavier, sticky, longer*). They learn the vocabulary associated with the scientific concepts they investigate. For example, in learning about plants, they may learn words such as *stem, roots, soil, dirt, buds,* and *petals.* Similarly, in learning about **habitats** of animals in their natural area, they may learn words such as *nest, ocean,* or *shelter.* Children also learn terms to refer to scientific procedures such as *observe, measure, predict, experiment,* and *discover.* The teacher models the use of such words across a variety of settings, and children gradually begin to use these words while engaged in inquiry (e.g., "I predict . . .," "Let me *check,*" "I *discovered* seeds inside.") (Gelman and Brenneman 2004; Gelman and others 2010). Scientific experiences also provide children with the context for using language and building communication skills, important aspects of language development for all children, including English learners and children with special needs.

The use of language extends and enriches scientific experiences and reinforces the growth of science content knowledge (Gelman and Brenneman 2004; Eshach 2006; Michaels, Shouse, and Schweingruber 2008). Interactions with adults and peers are crucial for the development of scientific ideas. The meaning of concepts is co-constructed—drawn from both adult and child language—with adults providing heavy scaffolding to facilitate the construction of knowledge and modeling language for the child. Children use language when they engage in conversations to share their findings and explanations and compare their own thinking with that of others. Furthermore, when co-creating scientific meaning, children learn that there is often more than one possible answer and that even their teacher may be unsure of the answer to the question under investigation. Research indicates that with adult guidance, three- and four-year-old children can engage in complex discussions involving observation, prediction, and explanation (Peterson and French 2008). Such discussions clarify children's ideas and develop their understanding of scientific phenomena (Jones, Lake, and Lin 2008). More important, guided discussion can foster children's attitude of inquiry and their willingness to share and discuss findings. Exposing children to "science talk" helps them to establish a pattern of "scientific conversations," which may assist in developing patterns of "scientific thinking" (Eshach 2006, 14).

In scientific explorations, children use different forms of communication to record and document information, from oral, signed, or written language (with adults' assistance) to drawings, photos, graphs, charts, logs, and maps. Documentation is helpful for facilitating the communication skills of children. Recording in journals provides opportunities for children to express their ideas in words, and an adult can transcribe, whether in English or in the child's home language, what children have to say. For example, children can use drawings and words to document the growth of their plant over time or the transformation of a caterpillar to a butterfly. The use of different forms of documentation is particularly helpful for facilitating the communication of children who are English learners and children with special needs. Children then have multiple ways to process information and express their ideas. Documenting information not only facilitates children's understanding of the concepts they learn, but it also provides a tool for communication. Children, guided by adults, can refer to their records at different times—for example, while discussing and sharing their observations and thoughts with others.

Scientific Knowledge: The Content of Science in Preschool

Another central assumption that guided the preparation of these foundations is that scientific content in preschool should be based on children's existing intuitive knowledge and interests related to science and on concepts children can explore directly in their everyday environment. Preschool children are predisposed to learn about different topics in science.

From a very young age, children have intuitive ideas or naïve (folk) theories about physics and biology (National Research Council 2000, 2007; Spelke 1990; Baillargeon 1995; Gelman 2003; Inagaki and Hatano 2002; Bullock, Gelman, and Baillargeon 1982). For example, they have a natural inclination and capacity to learn abstract concepts such as growth and motion. It is therefore reasonable to take advantage of children's predispositions and to base the content of preschool science on what children already know so that children can build on and expand their existing knowledge and understanding (National Research Council 2000, 2007; Gelman and Brenneman 2004; Gelman and others 2010). The content covered in the preschool science foundations includes core scientific ideas and concepts that, based on research, are developmentally appropriate for young children.

The foundations in each of the three strands (Physical Sciences, Life Sciences, and Earth Sciences) are organized around two unifying concepts in science: *properties and characteristics of objects* and *change*. The first substrand is about observing and exploring the properties and characteristics of objects: properties and characteristics of nonliving objects and materials (Physical Sciences), of living things (Life Sciences), and of earth materials and objects (Earth Sciences). Children investigate the inside and outside of objects, the **physical properties** (e.g., size, weight, shape, color, texture), the functions, and behaviors. In discovering the properties and characteristics of objects around them, children begin to recognize similarities and differences among objects and to categorize them based on different characteristics.

SCIENCE

The second substrand, or unifying concept, across the three strands of scientific content is *change*. Most things in nature are in the process of becoming different, or changing. All living things change over time through stages of the **life cycle** as they grow and develop, reproduce, and die. Changes occur in properties of materials (e.g., when solid materials are mixed with liquids) and in states of matter (e.g., from solids to liquids). Changes also occur in the position and motion of objects as objects are pushed, pulled, rolled, or dropped. Weather changes cause changes in the environment. According to Piaget, "knowledge develops through learning how objects move, how they change position and shape, and how they change in relation to themselves and other objects" (cited in Chaille and Britain 2002, 70).

Young children can notice, observe, and reason about some changes in objects and events. The second substrand in each of the three content strands is about change: changes in nonliving objects and materials (Physical Sciences), changes in living things (Life Sciences), and changes in the earth (Earth Sciences). The remainder of this chapter summarizes some of children's key early competencies in the areas of Physical Sciences, Life Sciences, and Earth Sciences. Bibliographic notes at the end of this section offer references to the research informing this chapter.

Physical Sciences: Early Concepts in Physics

The foundations in Physical Sciences are about investigating characteristics and physical properties of objects and materials, changes in objects and materials, and the motion of objects. Beyond the core list of foundations, young children can also investigate other concepts in physical sciences—for example, concepts related to sound as well as to light and shadows. At a very young age, children have a coherent set of concepts about the physical world. Piaget's theory of how physical knowledge is constructed emphasizes children's natural interest in examining objects, acting on them, and observing the object's reactions (Kamii and DeVries 1993). Through exploratory interactions with objects and adult guidance and support, young children learn about the physical properties of objects (size, shape, weight, texture, sound, flexibility, and rigidity) and the language to describe objects and their properties. They also explore different materials (solid and nonsolid **substances**) such as sand, milk, and play dough and learn about their inherent properties. Young children have distinct concepts about size and weight and learn words (*heavier, smaller,* and *larger*) to describe and compare these parameters. They understand weight mostly in terms of "felt weight," how heavy an object feels. Four- and five-year-olds also develop the concept of kinds of material (glass, plastic, wood, paper) and can distinguish between the identity of the objects (a cup), the materials objects are made of (plastic, glass), and parts of objects (Smith, Carey, and Wiser 1985).

Preschool children can also reason about changes and transformations of objects and materials. Some transformations involve the rearrangement of existing parts and structures to produce a new structure, such as when building with wooden blocks, play dough, and other construction materials. Other kinds of transformations involve changes in substance or consistency usually by combining and mixing materials, such as sand, dirt, water, paint, or the ingredients in cooking activities. Preschoolers know that objects cut into pieces are no longer the same kind of objects but are still the same materials (Smith, Carey, and Wiser 1985). A paper cup cut into pieces is no longer a paper cup, but it is still the same material. They also appreciate that a substance such as sugar continues to exist even after it has become invisible upon dissolving in water (Au 1994).

One immediate and visible way in which children interact with the physical world involves the movement of objects. Children's play involves the movement of their own body and of other objects in their environment. Throwing balls, pushing toy cars, rolling wheeled toys, and riding bikes are experiences in which preschool children produce movement by their own actions. Through such experiences, children discover the relationship between objects' physical properties (weight, size) and objects' motion and gain critical feedback about cause-and-effect relationships involved in everyday physics. They know that physical objects have to contact other objects to set them in motion and that physical effects require the transmission of force. For example, they can reason about the kind of mechanism (such as pulling, pushing, or rolling) that may or may not produce a certain outcome. In describing and reasoning about such experiences, children also learn the vocabulary to describe the speed, the direction, and the ways

things move—an effective way to expand the vocabulary of all children, including English learners.

Life Sciences: Early Concepts in Biology

The foundations in Life Sciences are about core concepts related to properties and characteristics of living things and their growth and change over time. The foundations focus on children's ability to actively explore, observe, and study the characteristics of animals and plants in the everyday environment, including appearances (insides and outsides), body parts, behaviors, habitats, and the changes and growth of living things over time.

One basic and important understanding of the biological and physical world is the distinction between animate objects (animals, people) and inanimate objects (nonliving objects and plants). Young children can distinguish between animate and inanimate objects on the basis of appearance, the capacity for independent action (such as walking or sitting), and the experience of psychological states (the ability to remember, feel happy, or express fear) (Gelman, Spelke, and Meck 1983). Children also differentiate between animals and inanimate objects on the basis of the insides. They expect animate objects to have blood and bones on the inside and inanimate objects to have materials, such as wood, cotton, and mechanical parts (Gelman 1990). They understand that animate objects have internal properties that enable them to move on their own and that inanimate objects cannot move themselves but must be propelled into action by an external force (Massey and Gelman 1988).

Young children have intuition about the essential properties of living objects and can distinguish them from nonliving objects (Gelman 2003). Children's intuitive understanding of living things is affected by their day-to-day experiences with the natural world and the cultural beliefs in their communities (Waxman and Medin 2006, 2007). The Bibliographic Notes expand on current research about cultural differences in children's reasoning about biological concepts. In general, by the age of five, children begin to grasp the commonalities between animals and plants despite the differences in appearance (Inagaki and Hatano 1996). They recognize that both animals and plants, but not artifacts, can grow and increase in size over time, heal through regrowth when damaged, and die (Rosengren and others 1991; Hickling and Gelman 1995; Backscheider, Shatz, and Gelman 1993; Nguyen and Gelman 2002).

Children as young as three years old expect animals to change over time due to growth (get bigger, not smaller) and understand that living things undergo changes. By age five, children realize that animals can undergo metamorphosis (from a caterpillar to a butterfly) (Rosengren and others 1991). Children also recognize the nature of plant growth and the innate potential of seeds and understand some aspects of the life cycle of plants (Hickling and Gelman 1995). By four and a half years of age, for example, children claim that a seed taken out of an apple and planted will grow into an apple tree (Gelman and Wellman 1991).

Growth and taking in food or water constitute the core of young children's concept of living things (Ingaki and Hatano 2002). From a young age, they associate growth of plants and animals with feeding or watering. They expect events such as growth or metamorphosis to have inherent internal causes outside human control. For example, they associate the growth of plants with natural processes, such as sunshine and rain (Hickling and Gelman 1995; Gelman 2003). By studying and comparing the needs of different animals and plants, children begin to realize that some needs (e.g., food, water, air) are basic to all living things and develop a greater understanding of the basic needs of living things—namely, humans, animals, and plants.

Earth Sciences: Early Concepts Related to Earth

The foundations in Earth Sciences are about actively exploring and investigating characteristics and physical properties of earth materials in the immediate environment and about observing and describing changes in the earth, including the movement and apparent changes of natural objects in the sky (e.g., sun, moon) and changes in the seasons and weather by using weather-related vocabulary (e.g., *sunny, cloudy, rainy, windy*). The Earth Sciences strand also includes a foundation about preserving the earth and children's awareness of the importance of caring for and respecting the environment.

Children have daily contact with many aspects of the earth—its soil, rocks, air and water, objects in the sky (such as the sun and the moon), and experiences of weather changes. Daily interactions and direct contact with objects and events in nature allow children to observe and explore the properties of earth materials and patterns of change in the world around them. For example, young children study the weather and seasonal changes in the environment, explore different kinds of soil and rocks, experiment with water, and track patterns of movement and change of the sun and the moon (Worth and Grollman 2003). Children's direct contact with the natural environment enhances their connection to nature and constitutes an essential and critical dimension of

healthy development (Kellert 2002). It also helps to raise their awareness of issues related to the care and protection of their own environment (Cohen and Horm-Wingerd 1993; Paprotna 1998).

Preschool children can notice, observe, and describe day/night, weather, and seasonal changes but are not ready to grasp scientific explanations for such earth phenomena. Research indicates that young children of different cultures start with a similar concept of the earth—one

Summary Table of Science Foundations

Strand	Substrand		Foundation
Scientific Inquiry	1.0	Observation and Investigation	1.1 1.2 1.3 1.4 1.5 1.6
	2.0	Documentation and Communication	2.1 2.2
Physical Sciences	1.0	Properties and Characteristics of Nonliving Objects and Materials	1.1
	2.0	Changes in Nonliving Objects and Materials	1.1
Life Sciences	1.0	Properties and Characteristics of Living Things	1.1 1.2 1.3 1.4
	2.0	Changes in Living Things	2.1
Earth Sciences	1.0	Properties and Characteristics of Earth Materials and Objects	1.1
	2.0	Changes in the Earth	2.1 2.2 2.3 2.4

SCIENCE

that is in conflict with current scientific theories. They initially believe that the world is flat (not a sphere). From a development perspective, the appropriateness of activities for young children that focus on learning about planets in space is highly questionable. Preschool children are not ready to grasp the idea that the earth spins around or that the earth moves around the sun (Kampeza 2006; Nussbaum and Novak 1976; Nussbaum 1979; Sneider and Pulos 1983). Therefore they cannot intuitively reason about everyday phenomena such as the day-and-night cycle and causes of weather. Nevertheless, observing and talking about day/night and seasonal changes form a foundation on which a more advanced concept of earth is developed in later years.

Scientific Inquiry

1.0 Observation and Investigation

At around 48 months of age	*At around 60 months of age*
1.1 Demonstrate curiosity and raise simple questions about objects and events in their environment.	**1.1** Demonstrate curiosity and an increased ability to raise questions about objects and events in their environment.
Examples	**Examples**
• Wondering why the toy car does not roll down the ramp, picks up the car and discovers that it is missing one wheel.	• When playing in the block area, creates a sloped ramp with blocks and rolls different toy cars down the ramp. Checks which car goes the farthest when rolling down the ramp.
• When building with blocks, puts more and more blocks on top to find out how tall the tower can get without falling apart.	• While digging in the mud, sees a worm and wonders, *Does it live in the ground? I see another one. Is it their home?* Another child observes the worm and asks, "Why does the worm not have eyes? How does it see to move?"
• Participates in preparing play dough, and asks, "How did it turn blue?"	
• Sees a snail and wonders, *Why is it hiding inside? When is it coming out?*	• On the playground, looks up and asks the teacher, "How come I can see the moon in the daytime?"
• A child who is nonverbal gestures to his friend to join in observing how the guinea pigs (the class pets) eat their food. He points, on his communication board, to the photo of a child eating and then points to the guinea pigs.	• Observes a ladybug in the yard and asks what would happen if she put it in a box with dirt and grass. Asks, "Can it be our class pet?"
	• While sorting different rocks, picks up one of the rocks and washes it with soap and water. Then gets the magnifying glass to observe it more closely.
• During lunchtime, mixes her sour cream with applesauce, and notices that sour cream changes its color. Then tries it out to find out what it tastes like.	• On a nature walk in the preschool yard, notices holes in the ground, points to the holes and calls out to get the teacher's attention, and asks, "What's there?"
• Picks up small "roly poly" bugs from under a rock and asks, "Why do they roll up in a ball?"	

SCIENCE

1.0 Observation and Investigation *(continued)*

At around 48 months of age	*At around 60 months of age*
1.2 Observe[1] objects and events in the environment and describe them.	**1.2** Observe objects and events in the environment and describe them in greater detail.
Examples	**Examples**
• Observes the inside and outside of a pumpkin by using different senses and describes how it looks, smells, and feels. Communicates to a bilingual assistant, "It has many seeds. It is soft inside."	• Observes a sweet potato growing in a jar, indicates the buds and roots, and may also communicate, "There are white roots going down and small leaves." Takes a photograph of the sweet potato, with the teacher's assistance, to document its growth.
• Observes a cylinder rolling down the slide and communicates, "Look, how fast it is rolling. Let me try it again."	• On a rainy day, participates in observing rain by using all senses and describes what the raindrops look like and how they feel, sound, smell, and taste. Records her observations through drawings and dictations in her journal.
• Tastes a piece of red apple and a piece of green apple and describes what they taste like.	
• A child with a visual impairment touches the bark of a tree and communicates, "It feels a little scratchy when I touch the bark."	• While exploring a rain stick, shakes it and listens to the sound it makes. Children share their observations: "I can hear something inside, like beans or small rocks"; "It sounds like rain"; "It looks like a long stick"; "It is made of wood"; "It has a drawing on it with many colors."
• After dropping different balls onto the floor, listens to and compares the different sounds they make. Indicates which ball makes a loud sound and which ball makes a soft sound.	• A child with visual impairments manipulates seashells on the sand table and describes what she touches: "It's bumpy and round," or "It's smooth and flat."
• On a walk around the neighborhood or schoolyard, squats down to smell some blooming flowers and tells a another child, "It smells so good!"	• Observing a snail closely, describes it: "It is hard like a rock. Its body looks very soft." Another child comments, "It moves very, very slowly. It has two long pointy things (antennas) sticking out."
• Observes a quilt she brought from home and describes the different fabrics of the squares (e.g., silk, flannel, corduroy) and textures (e.g., soft, furry, rough, smooth).	• A child with a speech delay draws a picture of the praying mantis inside the terrarium. When describing her drawing to the teacher, the child attempts to use words and points to her drawing and to the praying mantis. The teacher models words and the child nods her head yes and says, "praying mantis."
	• Observes the caterpillar (or a picture of a caterpillar) closely and draws a picture of a caterpillar in her journal. Communicates, "It has stripes—yellow, white, and black—like a pattern."

1. Other related scientific processes, such as classifying, ordering, and measuring, are addressed in the foundations for mathematics.

SCIENCE

1.0 Observation and Investigation *(continued)*

At around 48 months of age	*At around 60 months of age*
1.3 Begin to identify and use, with adult support, some observation and measurement tools.	**1.3** Identify and use a greater variety of observation and measurement tools. May spontaneously use an appropriate tool, though may still need adult support.
Examples	**Examples**
• While exploring, studying, or examining leaves, uses a magnifying glass, with the teacher's assistance, to observe a leaf closely.	• Asks for a magnifying glass to observe a worm more closely and communicates, "I need the magnifying glass to look very close."
• In a soil investigation, a child with a disability uses an adaptive shovel to collect soil in the yard.	• Fascinated with the growth of her green beans, a child points to the ruler and says to her teacher, "I want to see how big it is."
• Before going on a nature walk, the teacher handed children some observation tools. One child points to her hand lenses and tweezers and communicates, "We are going to look for very small creatures."	• While investigating worms, a child with a physical disability uses hand lenses fitted with a bigger grip to observe worms closely.
• Refers to the measuring tape and shares with his teacher that his father also uses the measuring tape at home.	• Uses tweezers to group small things found in soil.
• Using a measuring cup, helps the teacher measure two cups of flour during a cooking activity.	• While preparing dough, child uses a measuring cup to pour one cup of flour.
• While observing ants with a magnifier, says, "Look how big the seed is. It is bigger than the ant."	• Uses an eyedropper to add a few drops of food color to a mixture of glue and water.
	• Uses a balance scale to find out which apple is heavier and gestures to the lower pan of the scale to indicate it is heavier.
	• In the block area, child stacks blocks to his height and counts the blocks to measure his height.

SCIENCE

1.0 Observation and Investigation *(continued)*

At around 48 months of age	*At around 60 months of age*
1.4 Compare and contrast objects and events and begin to describe similarities and differences.	**1.4** Compare and contrast objects and events and describe similarities and differences in greater detail.
Examples	**Examples**
• Observes rocks and sorts them by size, indicating which are big and which are small.	• Observes plants in pots and communicates, "This one (indicating the one watered) is bigger, and the leaves are green. But this one did not grow. The leaves are yellow and soft. It looks dead."
• Using different senses, observes a watermelon, contrasts the inside and outside, and communicates: "The outside is green and hard, and the inside is red and soft."	• Observes different kinds of squash by using sight and touch and communicates similarities and differences: "These are more round, but this is long. This squash is yellow and green and is very smooth, but that one feels bumpy."
• When trying to roll different objects down the slide, demonstrates that the ball can roll down, but the block slides and does not roll.	• Contrasts the objects that can roll down a ramp (e.g., balls, marbles, wheeled toys, cans) with objects that cannot roll down (a shovel, block, book). For example, refers to objects that can roll down and communicates, "These are round and have wheels."
• Sees images in a picture book and describes her observation: "Frogs are green, and toads are brown."	
• Demonstrates how the truck is very slow and the yellow car is very fast.	• Contrasts a butterfly with a caterpillar (while observing pictures or actual objects); for example, communicates that the butterfly can fly and the caterpillar cannot and that the butterfly has a different shape and different colors.
• Compares a hummingbird egg to a chicken egg (while observing pictures or actual objects) and describes their similarities: "They are round and white and look the same."	• Observes and describes what the sky looks like on a foggy day and how it is different on a sunny day.
• A child with a speech delay dips his fingers in cups of water and indicates which cup has colder water.	• Compares creases in the palm of his hand to a leaf and communicates, "They both have stripes all over. Some lines are tiny, and some are long, like this one."
• While eating a tangerine during snack time, comments, "This tangerine doesn't have seeds. One time I ate a tangerine, and it had so many seeds."	• When working in the garden, uses a real shovel and describes how it is similar to or different from the toy shovel in the sandbox area.
	• Uses a piece of yarn to find out, with adult assistance, which of two pumpkins is larger.

SCIENCE

1.0 Observation and Investigation *(continued)*

At around 48 months of age	*At around 60 months of age*
1.5 Make predictions and check them, with adult support, through concrete experiences.	**1.5** Demonstrates an increased ability to make predictions and check them (e.g., may make more complex predictions, offer ways to test predictions, and discuss why predictions were correct or incorrect).

Examples	**Examples**
• Explores an apple and makes a prediction: "Maybe it has six seeds inside." After the teacher cuts it open, counts the seeds.	• After planting sunflower seeds, communicates, "The seeds will grow, and there will be sunflowers." Then, observes the plant daily for changes.
• When asked to predict, "What will happen if we mix the water with red," points to a cup with red liquid. Then tests his prediction by adding food color to a glass of water.	• In response to the question "What do you think will happen if water is added to the flour?" predicts, "The flour will feel sticky and will not look like flour anymore. The water and the flour will mix together." Another child suggests, "Let's pour some water and see what happens."
• Looks through the window on a windy day and predicts, "More leaves will fall down."	• Cuts open a tomato (which, by scientific definition, is considered a fruit), observes what it looks like inside and comments, "I thought there would be no seeds inside the tomato, but now I see tiny seeds inside."
• A child makes a prediction about how far the toy car will travel down the ramp by indicating the distance with a gesture. Then he pushes the car down to test his prediction.	
• Predicts that the dark green object has "gooey stuff" inside.	• At the sandbox, child predicts that if sand is poured over the spinning wheel, the wheel will spin, communicating: "It also turned when I poured water on it."
• Predicts that the worm will move if it is touched. The teacher replies, "Let's touch the worm gently and see what it does."	• While participating in an experiment to test the effect of sunlight on plants, predicts, "The plant near the window will grow, and the plant in the closet will die."
• After making a prediction about which block is heavier, uses the balance scale to test her prediction.	• Brings an object to the water table and predicts whether it will sink or float. Then puts the object in water and observes what happens. Comments to his friend, "Yes, I knew it! It is floating."
• As part of investigating different seeds, observes a coconut, and makes predictions about what is inside. Then says, "Now let's crack it and see what's inside. Let's taste it."	

SCIENCE

1.0 Observation and Investigation *(continued)*

At around 48 months of age	*At around 60 months of age*
1.6 Make inferences and form generalizations based on evidence.	**1.6** Demonstrate an increased ability to make inferences and form generalizations based on evidence.
Examples	**Examples**
• Looks outside the window and observes the trees moving. Infers that it is windy outside: "Look at the trees, it is windy!" • Notices that a plant is wilted and says that it needs some water. • Observes that the soil outside is wet and communicates, "It rained last night." • Observes the pet rabbit eating and communicates," It must be very hungry." • Walks into the room, smells the aroma of muffins from the kitchen, and says, "Mmm, did someone make muffins?"	• Observes many different fruits and vegetables and communicates that fruits have seeds and vegetables do not. • Observing the toy cars going down the ramp, infers that they go down fastest when the ramp is smooth. • Observes plants in highly lit and dimly lit locations in the room and communicates that plants need light to grow. • Observes a picture of an unfamiliar animal. Notices the wings and communicates, "It is a bird. I know it, because it has wings." • Observes a picture of a child dressed in a jacket, a scarf, mittens, and a hat and communicates that it must have been very cold outside.

2.0 Documentation and Communication

At around 48 months of age	At around 60 months of age
2.1 Record observations or findings in various ways, with adult assistance, including pictures, words (dictated to adults), charts, journals, models, and photos.	**2.1** Record information more regularly and in greater detail in various ways, with adult assistance, including pictures, words (dictated to adults), charts, journals, models, photos, or by tallying and graphing information.
Examples	**Examples**
• "Records" in her journal what the pumpkin looks like on the inside and draws an orange oval with many dots inside. The teacher writes down the child's observation in the home language: "It is soft inside and has lots of seeds." • Observes the weather and records on a group chart, using picture cards, whether it is sunny, rainy, or windy outside. • In collaboration with friends, creates a collage with rocks and leaves collected during a walk around the yard or neighborhood, and refers to it when describing the items collected on their walk. • Refers to a photo of herself when she was a baby when talking about how much she grew. • A child who is nonverbal records, on a flannel-board with flannel cutouts representing different food items, the kinds of food he ate for snack at group time. • Observes some silkworms raised in the classroom terrarium and comments, "They are always on the leaves!" Draws a picture of the silkworm and the leaf in her journal.	• "Records" in his journal, by gluing photos of the lima beans before they sprouted and after sprouting, how they grew. Describes the growth of lima beans. • Collects information by using tally marks to find out how many children have pets and how many do not have pets. • After observing the sky, records in her journal what the moon looked like by drawing a picture of the moon in the shape of a banana. Describes her drawing, and the teacher writes down her words. • After coming back from a walk in the neighborhood, creates with other children a model of a building they observed, using different materials such as boxes of different sizes, paper rolls, and plastic bottles. • A child with a physical disability draws a picture of the leaf she observed, using a thick or adapted crayon, and dictates a description to the teacher: "The leaf has a little cut in it. It has a lot of lines." • After an investigation of fruits and vegetables, records on a chart with other children which foods have seeds inside and which ones do not. They glue pictures of different fruits on one side of the paper and pictures of vegetables on the back.

SCIENCE

SCIENCE

2.0 Documentation and Communication *(continued)*

At around 48 months of age	*At around 60 months of age*
2.2 Share findings and explanations, which may be correct or incorrect, with or without adult prompting.	**2.2** Share findings and explanations, which may be correct or incorrect, more spontaneously and with greater detail.
Examples	**Examples**
• Building a tower with blocks, explains, "First I put the big blocks and then the small blocks. Now it does not fall." • A child with a language delay points to a big puddle in the yard, looks up to the sky and explains, "Rain." • Records the growth of a plant in the garden, and communicates, "The plant grew from a seed, just like the flower in the story." • Explains that the truck goes really fast because it has big wheels, even though it is an incorrect explanation. • Explains that soap is needed to make bubbles. • When asked, "What happened to the water?" explains, "It is hard now because we put it in the freezer."	• While mixing colors near the art table, explains that green resulted from mixing blue and yellow. • Explains that a plant turned brown because "we did not put it near the window like the other plant." • When talking about what is needed in order to grow, communicates, "We need food. The food goes into the stomach and then it makes us strong and helps our body to grow." • When talking with children about why they think some things slid faster and others slower when letting go of them at the top of the slide, children come up with different explanations: "It got stuck because it is heavy," "It is slippery," "It is bumpy," "It has wheels." • Observing the leaves and twigs on the ground, explains that the wind was strong and blew all the leaves and twigs down. • When asked whether a puppet can eat, explains, "A puppet cannot eat because it does not have a real mouth. You can draw him a mouth, but it is not real like this" (points to own mouth).

Physical Sciences

1.0 Properties and Characteristics of Nonliving Objects and Materials

At around 48 months of age	*At around 60 months of age*
1.1 Observe, investigate, and identify the characteristics and physical properties of objects and of solid and nonsolid materials (size, weight, shape, color, texture, and sound).	**1.1** Demonstrate increased ability to observe, investigate, and describe in greater detail the characteristics and physical properties of objects, and of solid and nonsolid materials (size, weight, shape, color, texture, and sound).

Examples	**Examples**
• Tries to push a toy car through a maze and realizes that the car is too big and cannot go through. Gets a smaller car and tries again. • Holds a wood block and a foam block. Refers to the wood block when asked which one is heavier. • While making a maraca, discovers that filling it with sand makes a softer sound and filling it up with pebbles makes a louder sound. • Builds a cave with assorted blocks and communicates, "You need to put the cardboard blocks first. They are bigger." • Playfully discovers what sinks and what floats. For example, puts a leaf in the water and communicates, "The leaf is not going down." • Balances a tower made of empty milk cartons and wooden blocks. Uses the milk cartons on top and the wooden blocks on the bottom "because these are more strong." • Participates in making a collage using materials of different textures (sandpaper, paper cloth, ribbons, rocks, sand, feathers) and describes each material: "The sandpaper feels rough, but the ribbon feels smooth." • Digs in the sandbox and communicates, "The sand is hot over there, but here it is cold." • Connects several clear tubes near the water table and gets excited when discovering how to manipulate the tubes to make the water flow faster. • Explains, after preparing applesauce, that applesauce tastes like an apple, but it looks very different: "It is soft, and you have to eat it with a spoon."	• Plays a game in which she describes characteristics of an object she has brought from home, and the group guesses what object is in the bag. For example, communicates, "It is round, it is shiny, you can play with it." • Uses a balance scale to find out which of two balls is heavier. • Observes two different xylophones by using her senses (sight, hearing, touch) and describes the similarities and differences: "This one is made of wood and is more heavy," "They sound different," "This one is more loud," "This one has many colors, and this one does not." • Blows with a straw on different objects such as a pencil, a piece of paper, a ball, a feather, and a leaf and tries to make them move. With assistance, records which objects moved and which did not by gluing pictures of the objects on a large piece of paper. • Tests and sorts objects (e.g., wood blocks, paper, clear plastic cups, aluminum foil) based on whether they are opaque or transparent. Gestures to the teacher and demonstrates how she can see through a plastic cup, "I can see you." The teacher replies, "You can see through the cup. The plastic cup is transparent." • During a cooking activity, explores sugar, flour, salt, powdered gelatin, or cornstarch by using the senses (touch, smell, and taste). Children communicate their observations: "All of them are white," "The flour is very soft," "The sugar looks more like salt, but it tastes sweet."

SCIENCE

1.0 Properties and Characteristics of Nonliving Objects and Materials *(continued)*

At around 48 months of age	At around 60 months of age
Examples	**Examples**
	• Working with clay, notices its similarities to play dough and communicates, "It is soft, and you can make different things with it just like with play dough, but you have to press it harder with your fingers."
	• After participating in making orange juice and lemonade, describes what each juice tastes like and participates in a discussion, guided by the teacher, of how the orange juice and lemonade are similar or different. After listening to the story of the three little pigs, holds a piece of straw, stick, and brick, and says, "The wolf can't blow the brick house down because it is stronger."

2.0 Changes in Nonliving Objects and Materials

At around 48 months of age	*At around 60 months of age*
2.1 Demonstrate awareness that objects and materials can change; explore and describe changes in objects and materials (rearrangement of parts; change in color, shape, texture, temperature).	**2.1** Demonstrate an increased awareness that objects and materials can change in various ways. Explore and describe in greater detail changes in objects and materials (rearrangement of parts; change in color, shape, texture, form, and temperature).
Examples	**Examples**
• At a painting easel, mixes red paint and yellow paint and communicates to her friend, "Look, it turned orange."	• While participating in making pancakes, describes what happens when the flour, milk, and eggs are all mixed together, commenting, "Let's add more milk and see what happens."
• Comments on changes from cream to butter after shaking cream in a jar: "Look, it's a ball."	• While making lemonade, mixes water with lemon juice and makes a prediction about how it is going to taste.
• Participates in making guacamole and demonstrates how she can make it soft by pressing and mixing the avocado with a fork.	• While experimenting with water, discovers that water "soaks in" when poured on a piece of sponge or paper towel, but not when poured on a plastic plate.
• Notices that the ice in the cup melted into water. Puts his fingers in the water, and gestures to the teacher to come over and feel the water.	• Records in her journal how the ice in the bowl melted: "I touched it with my finger, and it was very cold and very hard." The teacher asks, "What happened to the ice after lunch was over?" The child describes her drawing: "The ice was very small, and there was water in the bowl." The teacher writes the child's words down and rephrases the child's description: "Yes, the ice has melted."
• Notices how paper soaked in water changes: "It gets very mushy." "It breaks when I lift it up." His friend squeezes the soaked paper and communicates, "Look, the water comes out."	
• A child comments, "Yeah . . . bubbles," after the teacher added soap to the water table. The child points to the soap and communicates, "Put more soap. Pleeease! I want more bubbles."	• Notices that the play dough became hard and communicates, "Because we left it out all night."
• While playing with clay, communicates to her friend, "Let's smooth it first and make a pancake" and begins flattening the clay with the palms of her hand. Her friend pokes holes in it, using her finger, and then makes it flat again.	• In response to a question of what will happen if blue powder is added to water, children predict, "The water will turn blue," "The water and the paint will mix together, and it will be blue paint." Another child suggests, "Let's pour some paint in the water and see what happens."
• While playing with blue and yellow play dough, observes that the mixture became green and communicates, "Hey, teacher, I made green."	• Constructs an airplane by using pipe cleaners and communicates to his friend, "I made an airplane, but now I am going to make something else." The child converts it into a spaceship by tweaking and bending the pipe cleaners and rearranging their configuration.
	• After putting different-color crayons on top of a hot plate, the teacher has asked, "What do you think might happen?" Children predict, "It will get burned, it will get hot, and then they will mix."

SCIENCE

SCIENCE

2.0 Changes in Nonliving Objects and Materials *(continued)*

At around 48 months of age	*At around 60 months of age*
2.2 Observe and describe the motion of objects (in terms of speed, direction, the ways things move), and explore the effect of own actions (e.g., pushing pulling, rolling, dropping) on making objects move.	**2.2** Demonstrate an increased ability to observe and describe in greater detail the motion of objects (in terms of speed, direction, the ways things move), and to explore the effect of own actions on the motion of objects, including changes in speed and direction.

Examples	Examples
• While playing bowling in the yard, demonstrates to his friend, how to roll the ball hard to get it to the end. • Directs a small toy boat on the water table and pushes harder, on bumping into obstacles, "to make it go over the bumps." • Excitedly comes up with the idea of using the wagon to move a stack of blocks. Puts the blocks in a wagon and pulls the wagon from one area of the yard to another. • Makes a prediction about where the toy truck will stop after rolling down the ramp. • Blows through a straw on a Ping-Pong ball and discovers that it makes the ball move. • Plays with a train and describes how it moves: "It starts here and goes round and round like this. And then comes back." • A child with a new wheelchair demonstrates to her peers how she uses the ramp to go up and down instead of using the stairs. • Understands the effect of peddling a tricycle faster and says, "Look, teacher. Watch me go faster. I push the pedals harder."	• While rolling balls down the slide, refers to the steeper slide and communicates in the home language: "This one is faster. Look how fast this ball rolls down." • While playing with toy cars, notices that it is easier to move them on the floor and communicates to his friend, "Let's move over there. Cars go faster than on the carpet." • Observes a toy train going slowly on the tracks and tries different ways to make it go faster; for example, empties one of the cars or removes some of the cars. • After throwing the ball again, communicates to the teacher, "Now I threw it even more far. Let's measure how far." They measure the distance between the child and the ball and record it on a chart. • Observes a feather falling and describes, "It falls down very slowly. It does not fall straight down. It goes from side to side until it drops." • A child in a new wheelchair discovers that it is more difficult to roll on a carpet than on the floor and that he cannot roll on sand: "If I roll into the sand, I'll get stuck." • Places two toy cars at the top of a ramp and releases them at the same time. Observes which one reaches the bottom first.

Life Sciences

1.0 Properties and Characteristics of Living Things

At around 48 months of age	*At around 60 months of age*
1.1 Identify characteristics of a variety of animals and plants, including appearance (inside and outside) and behavior, and begin to categorize them.	**1.1** Identify characteristics of a greater variety of animals and plants and demonstrate an increased ability to categorize them.
Examples	**Examples**
• After cutting open a variety of fruits and discovering seeds inside, begins to recognize that fruits have seeds. When asked to predict what is inside an apricot, a child points to a seed and says "seed."	• Sorts fruits, such as mangoes, avocados, apples, grapes, peaches, and apricots, based on whether they have one seed or many seeds inside. Points to the avocado and apricot and says in the home language, "Look! They both have one big seed."
• Observes a squirrel climbing up the tree and notices that it has a long tail.	• During circle time, shares that one night they saw opossums in their yard.
• On a nature walk in the neighborhood or school-yard, identifies short plants and tall plants. A child who is an English learner points to or indicates a eucalyptus tree nearby and communicates, "Big tree."	• Observes and identifies the characteristics of a ladybug (e.g., its shape, size, colors, and how it moves) and shares observations with others when prompted by the teacher: "The ladybug is round and has tiny legs. It has black dots."
• When observing and identifying characteristics of a ladybug, a child comments, "The ladybug is very small." The child records in his journal his observation of the ladybug by drawing a picture of what it looks like. The child may dictate his observation to an adult.	• Observes plants and identifies the different parts (e.g., root, stem, buds, leaves).
• Looks at an informational book and identifies which animals can fly.	• While observing images of a variety of ducks on the computer, recognizes that ducks come in different colors.
• Sorts leaves, making piles of pointed and rounded leaf shapes, and communicates, "These are circle leaves, and these are pointy."	• Contrasts butterflies with moths and communicates that butterflies are more colorful and have bigger wings.
• Explores a variety of seeds and sorts them by size. Communicates, "These seeds are big, and these are very tiny."	• When talking about plant roots that we eat, one child says, "potatoes," another says, "taros," and another says, "yams."
• Observes a cactus and tells a friend, "They have needles. I got poked once."	

1.0 Properties and Characteristics of Living Things *(continued)*

At around 48 months of age	*At around 60 months of age*
1.2 Begin to indicate knowledge of body parts and processes (e.g., eating, sleeping, breathing, walking) in humans and other animals.[2]	**1.2** Indicate greater knowledge of body parts and processes (e.g., eating, sleeping, breathing, walking) in humans and other animals.
Examples	**Examples**
• After lunch, indicates his tummy and communicates, "I ate so much. My stomach is full." • Describes how his new sibling "sleeps all the time because he is still a baby." • Points to his head, and communicates in the home language, "My brain helps me think." • Touches her hand and presses on her skin when asked if she can feel her bones. • Points to a picture of an elephant in a book and tells another child, "Big poop! 'Cause they eat so much!" • Makes the connection between facial parts and senses (eyes for vision, ears for hearing). For example, covers her eyes and says, "Now I cannot see." • After running, touches his chest to feel his heart beating.	• When using a stethoscope in the dramatic play area, tells another child, "Look, when I breathe, my chest goes in and out." • Explains that when the caterpillar eats, the food goes to its stomach, and it poops. • After a discussion about body parts, rides the bicycle and communicates, "I am using the muscles in my arms and my legs." • Participates in a discussion about the outside and inside of the body. Touches his arms and communicates, "I can feel my skin, and inside my body I can feel my muscles and bones." • When asked, what is inside the body of the hen, predicts that there is blood, bones, and a heart inside. • After a physical activity, sits back in her chair and says, "I jumped so much. I feel my heart." • Explains, "We can walk with our legs, and birds fly with their wings."

2. The knowledge of body parts is also addressed in the *California Preschool Foundations (Volume 2)* for health. In science, it also includes the knowledge of body processes. Knowledge of body parts is extended to those of humans and other animals.

1.0 Properties and Characteristics of Living Things *(continued)*

At around 48 months of age	*At around 60 months of age*
1.3 Identify the habitats of people and familiar animals and plants in the environment and begin to realize that living things have habitats in different environments.	**1.3** Recognize that living things have habitats in different environments suited to their unique needs.

Examples	**Examples**
• Carefully digs in the mud, excitedly looking for worms or bugs. • While playing in the yard, observes a squirrel climbing up the tree and communicates, "I saw a squirrel in my yard. It lives in a tree." • On a walk around the neighborhood or school-yard, the teacher directs the child's attention to a bird nest. The child comments, "A bird lives there. Where is the bird?" • Draws a picture of her home and describes who lives in it: "Grandma, dad, mom, and me." • While looking at a picture book of different animals, demonstrates with his body how the fish and the dolphins swim in the ocean. • A child who is visually impaired holds a worm and says, "Where is the dirt? I want to put him back." • On a neighborhood walk, children come across a hole in the ground. Although one child attempts to step on it, another child says, "Don't step on it. A gopher lives there."	• Shares that on his trip to visit his grandma, who lives in the desert, he saw many cactuses. Explains, "The cactuses live in the desert." • After the rain, picks up a stick and stirs a puddle to look for worms. Explains, "I know they live there because one time I saw worms coming out." • Participates in building a nest. Using tweezers, collects twigs and leaves in the yard: "Just like birds use their beaks." • Explains that she lives in an apartment, but her aunt lives in a house. • Observes a spider in its web and explains, "The spider has a web so it can catch food." • Sorts photos of animals according to those living in water, those living on land, and those who can live in both the water and on the land. • A teacher who just returned from a nature trip shares photos of his experiences. In one of the photos, he is standing next to a pond. The children ask, "Did you see frogs?" "Were there any fish?" • In the course of a conversation about the habitats of different animals, child says, "The sea lion lives in the ocean, and the bear lives in a cave."

SCIENCE

1.0 Properties and Characteristics of Living Things *(continued)*

At around 48 months of age	At around 60 months of age
1.4 Indicate knowledge of the difference between animate objects (animals, people) and inanimate objects. For example, expect animate objects to initiate movement and to have different insides than inanimate objects.	**1.4** Indicate knowledge of the difference between animate and inanimate objects, providing greater detail, and recognize that living things (humans, animals, and plants) undergo biological processes such as growth, illness, healing, and dying.
Examples	**Examples**
• While in the yard, points to a ladybug and tells his friend, "It is a real one! Look, it's moving."	• Communicates, "This roly-poly is alive. It looks like a little ball when I hold it in my hand, but when I put it on the ground it starts moving."
• Does not expect his toy puppy to move around. When asked, explains, "It doesn't have real legs."	• Shares with his teacher, "My puppy is sick. We took him to the vet to check his heart and bones, and the doctor gave him medicine."
• Communicates, "It won't hurt you, teacher; it's not real," while wiggling a wooden snake at teacher's leg.	• When asked whether the toy rabbit can actually run, replies, "This rabbit is just a pretend rabbit. It can't really run."
• Communicates that a toy cat cannot eat because "it is not real" and explains, "It has soft stuff inside."	• After listening to a story, explains," Of course this story is not real, because trees can't really talk and walk."
• While observing a snail, communicates, "It only looks like a rock, but it has a head and can move."	• While playing in the yard, a child hits a bush and a flower falls off. The child communicates, "It will grow again."
• Puts a toy fish in a bowl of water and communicates, "It does not swim in the water like this fish (points to the one in the aquarium) because it is not real."	• Holds a broken doll and communicates, "We need to fix it." However, for a living thing, may communicate, "My friend broke his arm. He has to wear a cast for a lot of days, until his bone gets better."
• Communicates, "My puppy is going to get big, but this one (showing toy) won't."	• Communicates, "I had a goldfish, but one day it got very sick and died."

2.0 Changes in Living Things

At around 48 months of age	*At around 60 months of age*
2.1 Observe and explore growth and changes in humans, animals, and plants and demonstrate an understanding that living things change over time in size and in other capacities as they grow.	**2.1** Observe and explore growth in humans, animals, and plants and demonstrate an increased understanding that living things change as they grow and go through transformations related to the life cycle (for example, from a caterpillar to butterfly).
Examples	**Examples**
• Records in his journal, with adult assistance, a footprint. Compares it to a footprint from three months ago and communicates, "I am four. I have bigger feet now." • Observes the beans she is growing and makes a prediction about how tall they will grow. • Communicates, "Teacher, I'm big now. I can turn on the light." • Looks at a picture book and explains, "This is the horsey when it was a baby, and then it grew and became this big (indicating a picture of a bigger horse)." • Communicates, "My baby brother had no teeth, but now he has teeth." • Holds a baby shirt she has brought from home, and compares it with the shirt she is wearing, indicating how much she has grown. • Fascinated by how the silkworms spun their cocoons, asks, "How do they turn into cocoons?" • While singing and acting a song about "growth," pretends she is a plant and demonstrates with her body how the little seed grew into a seedling, and the seedling grew into a tree.	• Draws in her journal a picture of her plant and communicates to her teacher, "These are the seeds inside, and then they grew, and we saw the little leaves, and then the leaves grew more." • Observes tadpoles closely and communicates, "They are so much bigger now. Later the legs will come out. They will be frogs." • After planting the sunflower seeds, makes a prediction: "The seeds will grow, and there will be sunflowers." • Fascinated with the growth of the larvae (caterpillar) in the room, comments, "Oh, these are bigger. Maybe we should give the small ones more food." • Looks at the picture book *The Tiny Seed* and retells the story in his home language and some English, referring to pictures and describing how the seed grew into a plant. • Sees a picture of a Canada goose hatching eggs and asks, "How long does it take for the little geese to come out?" • Shows the group his baby photos he has brought from home and describes how he has grown and changed. • While observing a tub of silkworms, exclaims, "Look, one of the worms molted" while pointing at the silkworm's molted skin shell.

2.0   Changes in Living Things *(continued)*

At around 48 months of age	*At around 60 months of age*
2.2 Recognize that animals and plants require care and begin to associate feeding and watering with the growth of humans, animals, and plants.	**2.2** Develop a greater understanding of the basic needs of humans, animals, and plants (e.g., food, water, sunshine, shelter).
Examples	**Examples**
• While working in the garden, notices the dry soil and tries to water the flowers. • Collects grass and flowers in a cup. The teacher questions, "What will you do with your grass and flowers?" The child replies, "It is for my ladybug. It eats grass and flowers." • Observes the plant in the room and communicates, "We need to water it, so it grows bigger." • Communicates, "We need to eat breakfast to be strong and grow." • Helps take care of the class pet. While observing the class hamster, notices the food tray is empty and says, "Teacher, she needs some food!" • Communicates, "My baby sister was very little, but now she is big because she eats cereal." • Refers to a storybook and explains that the caterpillar ate a lot of leaves and became a butterfly.	• In an experiment with plants, children describe their observations: "The plants near the window grew, but the plants with no light became yellow." • Feeds the class pet fish, with adult assistance, and explains, "We give special food just for fish but not too much." • When planting bean seeds, the teacher asks, "What is needed for them to grow?" A child responds, "If you water it, it's going to grow more." Another child says, "They need soil." • Shares with his friends, "When we went to visit my aunt, someone came to my house every day to give my cat water and food, so he wouldn't be hungry." • After the rain, comments, "The plants must be so happy to drink so much rain." • After the butterflies have come out of the chrysalises, spontaneously discusses with other children plans to release the butterflies. • Helps his teacher add more soil to the potted plant and communicates, "It needs soil for food, and that's how it grows."

Earth Sciences

1.0 Properties and Characteristics of Earth Materials and Objects

At around 48 months of age	*At around 60 months of age*
1.1 Investigate characteristics (size, weight, shape, color, texture) of earth materials such as sand, rocks, soil, water, and air.	**1.1** Demonstrate increased ability to investigate and compare characteristics (size, weight, shape, color, texture) of earth materials such as sand, rocks, soil, water, and air.
Examples	**Examples**
• Observes different rocks collected on a nature walk (using the senses of sight and touch). Sorts out all the smooth rocks. • Plays with rocks and discovers that she can use a rock to draw on a sidewalk. • Fills a bucket with soil and comments, "We need water to make it more squishy." • While playing in the sandbox, pours sand into a bottle and communicates to his friend in his home language, "I can fill up the bottle with sand all the way up." • While outside, observes a windmill spinning. Responds, "I can feel the wind. The air is pushing it." • A child who is visually impaired holds different rocks and communicates, "This one feels really smooth, but this one is not very smooth." • Uses a magnifying glass to observe sand and communicates, "I can see many tiny pieces." • Explains that sand and water are needed to make a sand castle.	• Pours water on sand and compares the dry sand with the wet sand (e.g., "The wet sand sticks together"). Demonstrates how to make a cake with wet sand by filling up the bucket and then turning it over. • Pours water in the sandbox to form craters, lakes, and dams. • Investigates the surfaces of different rocks and sorts the rocks based on how shiny they are. Communicates, "Here are very shiny rocks, and here are not so shiny rocks." • In explorations of air, observes a kite flying and communicates, "The wind blows really hard, and the kite goes really high into the clouds." • Collects soil from the garden and uses a magnifying glass to observe the container of soil closely. Describes and records, with adult assistance, observations: "The soil has tiny rocks inside. The soil has some yellow leaves and some leaves that turned almost black. The soil is a little wet and feels very soft."

2.0 Changes in the Earth

At around 48 months of age	*At around 60 months of age*
2.1 Observe and describe natural objects in the sky (sun, moon, stars, clouds) and how they appear to move and change.	**2.1** Demonstrate an increased ability to observe and describe natural objects in the sky and to notice patterns of movement and apparent changes in the sun and the moon.
Examples	**Examples**
• Gestures toward the sky and communicates in the home language, "Last night I looked at the sky, and I saw the moon."	• Observes the sky and describes, "In the morning the sun was here, and now it moved over there. It is the same like yesterday."
• Participates in a class activity observing the sky and describing what the clouds look like. Communicates, "The sky is blue, and I see clouds. One cloud is small, and many clouds are big."	• Communicates, "When I looked at the sky with my dad, I saw the moon, and it was round and big. I saw the stars, too."
• Records his observation of the sky by drawing a picture. Refers to his drawing and indicates, or points to, the sun and the clouds.	• Shares in circle time with the group that the image on the moon one night looked like a rabbit. Other children disagree, saying it looked like a horse or a person.
• Communicates, "When I look at the sky at night, I see lots of stars."	• Communicates, "Sometimes, when I look at the sky at night, I see only the moon, and sometimes I see the moon and the stars."
	• Observes the moon and draws a representation of it in her journal. The child notices that it changes over time and communicates, "Now the moon is round and big, but sometimes it looks like a banana."
	• Observes the clouds on a rainy day and describes how they are different from those on a sunny day: "Sometimes the clouds are white, but today they are gray."
	• Says, "Last night I saw a full moon. Sometimes we eat mooncakes when there is a full moon."[3]

3. Some Asian families celebrate the Moon Festival by eating mooncakes.

SCIENCE

SCIENCE

2.0 Changes in the Earth *(continued)*

At around 48 months of age	*At around 60 months of age*
2.2 Notice and describe changes in weather.	**2.2** Demonstrate an increased ability to observe, describe, and discuss changes in weather.

Examples	Examples
• A child who is deaf/hearing impaired looks through the window and communicates in sign language, "It is raining." • Communicates, "It is windy. The wind is blowing my hair." • While playing outside, notices some raindrops, looks up, and starts singing a song about the rain. • Participates in a morning activity by recording the weather on a chart. Picks up the picture card with a drawing of sun to indicate that it is a sunny day. • Observes the weather and describes in his home language, "The sun is out. It is a sunny day." • Draws a picture of a rainbow and says, "It stopped raining. We went outside and saw a rainbow in the sky." • After the rain has stopped, checks how much water is in the bucket, trying to lift the bucket and look inside.	• Observes the weather and makes a prediction, "The sky is gray. I think it is going to rain." • Describes her observations of the wind by drawing in her journal how different objects (e.g., the trees, leaves, papers, and the flags) are blown by the wind. • Observes the chart with the daily recordings of the weather and communicates, "This week, it was sunny every day." • When it starts sprinkling outside, takes a can and walks outside, explaining, "I am taking the can to collect rain." • Observes and describes what the yard looks like on a rainy day and how it is similar or different from the yard on a sunny day.

2.0 Changes in the Earth *(continued)*

At around 48 months of age	*At around 60 months of age*
2.3 Begin to notice the effects of weather and seasonal changes on their own lives and on plants and animals.	**2.3** Demonstrate an increased ability to notice and describe the effects of weather and seasonal changes on their own lives and on plants and animals.
Examples	**Examples**
• In dramatic play area, pretends it is a rainy day, puts on boots and a coat, and carries an umbrella.	• Says or communicates, "We can't find bugs outside because it's cold, and they're hiding under the ground."
• On cold days, gets her jacket from her cubby before going outside. Explains, "I need my jacket because it is very cold."	• Communicates, "In the winter, I wear a jacket and in the summer when it is hot, I wear shorts."
• While observing the trees in the fall, describes, "The leaves are yellow and brown and falling down."	• While observing the trees in the yard, notices, "A lot of leaves fell down, but there are still some on the trees. The wind is going to blow them down, too."
• After the rain, notices the puddles in the yard. Excitedly gestures to his friend and says, "I am jumping in the water." The teacher comments, "It's fun splashing in a puddle. Let's see if we can find more puddles."	• Communicates, "Because of the storm, we could not go outside to play."
• Communicates, "It was raining, and I called my dog to come inside, so he does not get wet."	• On arrival in the morning, communicates, "It was so foggy. We couldn't see through the window."
• While playing outside on a sunny day, touches the slide and communicates, "The sun makes it hot, very hot."	• Around spring, observes the trees, records the growth of buds and new leaves, and communicates, "Look how many small leaves grew on the tree."
• During circle time, the teacher talks about how the leaves fall in autumn. Later, on a nature walk, a child points to some pine trees and asks the teacher, "How come those trees don't have leaves all around?"	• Notices snails on the sidewalk and explains that she saw them outside her house after the rain stopped.
	• Communicates to a friend in her home language, "Last night it was freezing outside. I put on my mittens because my hands were very cold."

SCIENCE

2.0 Changes in the Earth *(continued)*

At around 48 months of age	*At around 60 months of age*
2.4 Develop awareness of the importance of caring for and respecting the environment, and participate in activities related to its care.	**2.4** Demonstrate an increased awareness and the ability to discuss in simple terms how to care for the environment, and participate in activities related to its care.
Examples	**Examples**
• Helps the teacher to sort recyclable items such as papers, bottles, and cans. • Turns off the faucet after washing his hands. • Asks teacher if leftover fruit from lunch can be given to the class pet turtle. • When playing outdoors, remembers not to pick flowers from the garden. • Takes a turn in being the room's "light keeper" and turns off the lights when leaving the room to play outside.	• Uses recycling bins more independently. May remind another child to put a paper towel in the blue recycling box. • Reminds a friend to turn off the faucet "so we do not waste water." • Explains that when it is really hot, her mom puts the outdoor toys away to protect them from the sun. • Explains that at home the blue recycling bin is for the bottles, and the green can is for the leaves. Only the black garbage bin is for other trash. • After having a picnic in the neighborhood park, spontaneously helps the teacher to clean up the picnic area. • Shares with his teacher, "When I go with my mom to the park, I feed the birds."

SCIENCE

Bibliographic Notes

Traditionally, a commonly held notion about science education was that elementary and even middle school children lack the developmental readiness to engage in abstract reasoning—primarily the ability to evaluate evidence and to understand how evidence supports or contradicts theories or hypotheses (Dunbar and Klahr 1989; Inhelder and Piaget 1958; Schauble 1990). For preschool children, the common view was that their reasoning is concrete and perceptually based (Piaget 1952). However, more current research in cognitive development shows that young children are cognitively competent to engage in aspects of scientific inquiry processes and to learn basic scientific concepts about common phenomena of the natural world (Spelke 1990; Baillargeon 1995; Gelman 2003; Inagaki and Hatano 2002; Bullock, Gelman, and Baillargeon 1982; Brown 1990).

Scientific Inquiry

During the preschool years, children are developmentally ready to engage in scientific skills, such as observation, classification, comparing, and predicting (Gelman and Brenneman 2004; French 2004; Gelman and others 2010). Very young children actively observe objects and events in their environment. Observation involves the use of all the senses. Early on, infants and toddlers want to touch and handle objects and examine objects with their lips and tongues. They actively search for information about objects and events in their environment (Lind 1997). Through observations and by acting on objects, children learn about the physical characteristics of objects (size, shape, material, or weight), and how objects interact, move, and change. This information feeds children's growth in understanding concepts and acquiring knowledge in core domains such as biology and physics.

As children develop their inquiry skills, they can use prior knowledge and observable information to predict future events (Jones, Lake, and Lin 2008). Making a prediction is a cognitive skill that requires children to use existing knowledge and/or data that are immediately available and to predict new information. The extent to which children can accurately predict is related to their knowledge base and prior experiences. Research indicates that preschool children are capable of using their knowledge to make predictions for different natural phenomena. In domains in which young children have conceptual knowledge, their predictions tend to be relatively reasonable and accurate (Bullock, Gelman, and Baillargeon 1982; Inagaki and Hatano 2002; Zur and Gelman 2004).

The more experiences children have had with natural phenomena, the more likely they are to be able to accurately predict events related to the same phenomena. By testing and verifying their predictions, children gain new information that informs their future predictions. For example, when children were initially asked to predict the number of seeds in an apple, their predictions varied widely. However, with more experiences of predicting and verifying the number of seeds in an apple by counting the number of seeds, children's predictions became more accurate and reasonable over time (Gelman and Brenneman 2004).

Children's ability to make **inferences** is evident from a young age. Children can use the knowledge of natural kinds of categories (such as dog or bird) as the basis for novel inferences, knowing that members of a category share underlying properties. When four-year-old children were told a new fact about a particular dog, "that it has leukocytes inside it," they were likely to infer that other dogs have leukocytes inside them (Gelman and Markman 1986, 1987). Young children can also use observable evidence to make inferences or draw conclusions. Research indicates that they can make accurate inferences on the basis of relevant evidence. For example, very young children can infer causal relations and accurately conclude, based on patterns of evidence, what causes a machine to light up and play music (Gopnik and others 2001). They can make accurate causal inferences based on evidence, even when the evidence they observe contradicts their knowledge (Schulz and Gopnik 2004; Schulz, Bonawitz, and Griffiths 2007).

Young children are sensitive to evidence they observe. For example, they can recognize when evidence is uncertain. In a study by Schulz and Bonawitz (2007), preschool children showed a preference for playing with a toy that presented ambiguous evidence (a lever that sometimes did and sometimes did not cause an effect) over a familiar toy with expected manipulation. They engaged in more exploratory play when causal evidence was not consistent. Older children begin to demonstrate an understanding of the

relation between evidence and hypothesis. Five-year-olds can begin to use evidence correctly to form a hypothesis and modify their hypothesis according to new evidence (Ruffman and others 1993). By the early grades, children can also distinguish between a conclusive and an inconclusive test for a simple hypothesis (Sodian, Zaitchik, and Carey 1991).

Preschool children learn to use language to describe their observations and communicate their thoughts. Early childhood is a time of extensive vocabulary development (Anglin 1993). Observations and investigations provide an ideal opportunity to expose all children, including English learners, to new words and scientific vocabulary in English and in their home language, whenever possible.

Research indicates that science curriculum delivered in an early childhood education environment that is rich in language and opportunities for authentic communication with adults and peers leads to measurable improvements in children's language and supports children's acquisition of both the meaning and pragmatic aspects of language (French 2004). For children who communicate in alternative ways, such as in sign language, picture symbols, or other methods, scientific vocabulary is available as well.

The use of language to describe observations and other steps in the exploration process is an integral part of children's learning and formation of scientific concepts (Gelman and Brenneman 2004; Eshach 2006). Language extends and enriches scientific experiences and facilitates conceptual growth. For example, as children explore concepts such as growth, nutrition, or weather, they gradually

SCIENCE

learn the terms for the concepts they explore. The use of these terms, in turn, enriches their learning experiences. Children may also begin to use relevant scientific terms—for example, "I *observe*," "My *prediction* is," and "Let me *check*"—as they practice inquiry skills across a variety of settings (Gelman and Brenneman 2004). English learners, for whom the development of new vocabulary and language skills is most effective in authentic learning experiences, especially benefit. In the context of scientific explorations, children also learn to engage in complex discussions involving observation, prediction, and explanation (Peterson and French 2008). Such discussions develop children's understanding of the scientific phenomena they explore (Jones, Lake, and Lin 2008).

Physical Sciences

Young children learn about the physical world by observing and interacting with physical objects. They use all their senses to learn about the properties of different objects in their environment, including the color, size, shape, weight, smell, sound, texture, and, when appropriate, taste of objects. According to Piaget's theory, physical knowledge is constructed when children act on objects and observe the object's reactions, especially when reactions are observable and happen immediately. When variations in the child's action result in corresponding variations in an object's reaction, children have an opportunity to construct knowledge of corresponding events and to become aware of **cause-and-effect** relationships (Kamii and DeVries 1993; DeVries and others 2002).

Children approximately three and four years of age have distinct concepts of size and weight and learn distinct words to describe and compare these parameters (such as *larger, smaller* or *heavier*). In a study by Smith, Carey, and Wiser (1985) that traced the development of children's concepts of weight, size, density, and material kind, children focused on size (and ignored weight) when asked to explain physical phenomena related to size, such as which blocks will fit into a certain size box. However, they focused on weight and ignored the size of objects when explaining weight-relevant phenomena, such as "which blocks will make a foam rubber bridge collapse." Young children consider weight a physical property of objects, which causally affects that object's interaction with other objects. However, they typically understand weight in terms of "felt weight." They judge weights by lifting objects. They would insist that a tiny piece of polystyrene plastic (e.g., Styrofoam), for example, weighs nothing at all. They also do not have the consistent expectation that size can be a predictor of the heaviness of objects and may ignore size in predicting weight. Still, preschool children (i.e., three- to five-year-olds) can become engaged in weight-based problem solving such as in balancing the pans on a balance scale with a variety of materials. In the course of solving the problem, they construct possible solutions, closely examine the reaction of the pans, and gradually elaborate their understanding of how to balance the pans (Metz 1993).

Four- and five-year-old children also begin to develop the concept of kinds of materials and to distinguish kinds of materials (plastic) from the identity of objects (a cup) and parts of an object (handle). They respond with names of materials (e.g., wood, plastic) when asked about the kind of material the object is made of and are not misled into giving names of parts of objects (e.g., *leg, wing*) (Smith, Carey, and Wiser 1985). They also know that cutting can destroy objects but not affect the material the objects are made of. For example, they know that cut-up objects, such as paper or balloons, are no longer the same kind of objects but that they are still the same *kinds of materials*. At a young age, children know several words for kinds of materials (such as *glass* and *plastic*) and can state relevant properties of certain materials (for example, glass is breakable or plastic can be hard). However, their concept of density, a characteristic of kinds of material, is not developed until they are about eight years old. For example, three- and four-year-old children cannot distinguish between objects made of steel and objects made of aluminum. When asked which is made of a heavier kind of stuff, they make a judgment based on felt weight (Smith, Carey, and Wiser 1985).

Through daily interactions with all kinds of substances such as sand, play dough, milk, juice, dirt, and various kinds of food, children as young as age two explore how various substances differ in taste, smell, texture, and so on. They begin to differentiate and can learn names of various materials (Soja, Carey, and Spelke 1991; Prasada 1993). They also begin to form an intuitive sense about materials. One example of such intuition is that substances are **homogeneous**—for example, a spoonful of sugar picked up from one side of the pile or the other is still sugar. A study by Au (1994) indicates that by the age of three or four, children seem to believe that any portion of a substance is the same "kind" as the whole chunk or pile, even when it is in smaller chunks, ground up into a powder, or dissolved in water. For example, children appreciate that a substance such as sugar continues to exist even after it has become invisible upon dissolving. The notion of homogeneous structure in substances provides children a coherent basis for explaining why a substance maintains certain inherent properties as well as its identity, despite dramatic transformation into grain size or chunk size. However, young children have difficulty comprehending changes in state of matter, particularly reasoning about the transition from liquid to gas (Russell, Harlen, and Watt 1990).

Much of the understanding of the physical world rests on the ability to relate events causally and identify cause-and-effect relations. Research indicates that before infants can talk about objects, or even reach for objects and manipulate them, they can reason about how objects move and demonstrate an implicit understanding of the causal relations involved in everyday physics. In the first year, infants have an understanding that objects need support to prevent them from falling (Baillargeon, Needham, and DeVos 1992) and that objects cannot move through each other. They understand that objects cannot move themselves— that inanimate objects need to be propelled into action—and perceive causality in events (Leslie 1994; Oakes and Cohen 1990). This early understanding continues to evolve through children's spontaneous play and

SCIENCE

interactions with objects and becomes accessible and more explicit in a wider range of experiences during the preschool years.

Research indicates that at a very young age, children understand the causal relations involved in everyday physics. First, young children typically assume that physical events have a cause and intuitively search for a cause. They are also sensitive to the temporal ordering of cause-and-effect and believe that causes must precede their effects. Finally, young children can reason about the kind of mechanism that can or cannot produce a certain outcome (such as pulling, pushing, or rolling). For example, when observing a cause-and-effect event in which a ball rolled against a jack-in-the-box, children could reason about the cause and effect. They attributed the effect to the ball hitting the jack-in-the-box, presumably because rolling and hitting can produce movement in another object through impact. When asked to explain how an event occurred, some children generated mechanistic, physically oriented explanations (Bullock, Gelman, and Baillargeon 1982).

Life Sciences

The distinction between animate and inanimate objects is considered the most basic and important one for young children's understanding of the physical and biological world. It is believed that children's ability to distinguish between animate and inanimate objects is a foundation, or a precursor, to the ability to make the more general distinction between living and nonliving things (Inagaki and Hatano 2002).

Research indicates that children as young as three have an understanding of the difference between **animate** and **inanimate** objects. R. Gelman, Spelke, and Meck (1983) interviewed three- to five-year-old children with the use of animate and inanimate objects, such as a person, a cat, and a rock and inanimate objects with humanlike appearances, such as dolls or puppets. The interview included questions about the objects' appearance ("Does X have a head/stomach, feet, eyes, ears?"), the capacity for independent action ("Can X walk/sit?"), the potential for psychological states ("Can X think/ remember, feel happy, feel sad?"), and the tendency to engage in reciprocal activities ("Can X play with you/listen to, run with, kiss, hug?") (Gelman, Spelke, and Meck 1983, 300). They found that children as young as three years old made correct responses when asked about characteristics of animate and inanimate objects. Interestingly, there was no age difference in children's ability to distinguish between animate and inanimate objects. Although older children were more articulate and gave more explanations, their explanations did not differ in kind from those of younger children.

All children were eager to talk about this distinction between animate and inanimate objects and to justify their answers with relevant explanations. Children's answers to questions about a doll and a puppet, in particular, provided further evidence that preschoolers are not inclined to attribute animate characteristics to inanimate objects even when these objects can move or have an animatelike appearance. In a more recent study, using a similar interview method, Subrahmanyam, Gelman, and Lafosse (2002) demonstrated that four- and five-year-olds can also distinguish animate objects from machines, including machines that mimic an animate property such as a car or a robot, that seem to move on their own, or computers that appear to think and communicate. The children were more likely to attribute animate properties (such as talking, breathing, remembering, or thinking) to animate objects than to inanimate objects such as simple artifacts or machines. The only machine that was given the capacity to think and remember was a robot.

Young children can distinguish between animate and inanimate objects, even if the objects are unfamiliar, based on an object's capacity for self-initiated movement. Massey and Gelman (1988) presented three- and four-year-olds with photographs of unfamiliar objects, including mammals, an insect, statues with animal-like appearance, wheeled vehicles, and other multipart objects. They asked the children whether each of these objects could go up and down a hill by itself. Preschool children demonstrated an understanding that "real" animals could go up and down a hill by themselves, while inanimate objects, even if they looked like animals, could not (e.g., because "it's not a real piggy; it's just a furniture one" (Massey and Gelman 1988, 314). Children's causal explanations of how movement takes place differ between animals and inanimate objects. Young children understand that animate objects have the potential to move themselves because they are made of biological matter. Inanimate objects, on the other hand, are composed of nonbiological material, and the cause of inanimate motion is external to the objects and is

caused by agents and forces of nature (Gelman 1990). These principles direct young children when identifying an object and provide them with a coherent way to assimilate and process information about objects in their environment.

Young children also distinguish animates from inanimates on the basis of the inside of an object. They expect the insides of animals and inanimate objects to differ. When asked, "What is on the inside of X?" (Subrahmanyam, Gelman, and Lafosse 2002, 355), children thought that animate objects had blood and bones on the inside, but machines had buttons and knobs and other parts made of materials such as plastic and glass. Children understand that the insides of objects have a special status related to the object's identity and function (Gelman and Wellman 1991). By four years of age, they appreciate the special importance of insides for an object's identity and how it functions. They demonstrate an understanding that insides of objects have essence-like qualities. For example, if a horse is dressed like a zebra, children will judge its identity on the basis of the inside and not based on its external appearance. They will say it is still a horse (Keil 1989). However, in a study by Gelman (2003, 79), when children were asked to consider an "inside removal" of animals (e.g., "What if you take out the stuff inside of a dog. Is it still a dog?"), they claimed that removal of the insides changed the animal's identity and function. They recognize that if the inside of an object is removed, the identity and the function of an object would change (Gelman and Wellman 1991).

The broader distinction between **living things** (both animals and plants) and nonliving things is more challenging for young children. To make the distinction between living and nonliving things, young children need to view plants as biological entities and distinguish both plants and animals from nonliving things. This is difficult for young children primarily because plants and animals differ in outward appearance and in the capacity for self-generated movement and psychological states. They are similar only in dimensions relevant to biology.

In studies in which children were asked whether animals, plants, and inanimate objects were alive, preschool children had difficulty with the terms "living things" or "alive," and at ages four to five, they tended to interpret those terms as referring to animals, but not plants (Carey 1985; Richards and Siegler 1986). However, in studies that had children focus on particular features of living things such as growth, rather than the general question of whether an object is "alive," three- and four-year-old children could distinguish both animals and plants from nonliving objects.

Children's acquisition of the concept "alive" or "living things" is shaped by factors in their environment, including their everyday experiences, the language spoken by the child, and the cultural practices and beliefs in their community. Cultural differences in the understanding of the concept "alive" were evident in a study with children from Mexico, the United States, and Indonesia. Children in all three communities distinguished living things from nonliving things, recognizing that animals and plants grow and die. However, children revealed cross-cultural differences regarding the term *alive.* Children of the Mayan community,

in Mexico, tended to attribute life to certain natural objects (e.g., the sun, water)—items that are considered inanimate outside their community. English-speaking children interpreted *alive* as referring to humans and animals, but not plants. On the other hand, Indonesian-speaking children at a younger age than English-speaking children, attributed the term *alive* to both animals and plants. These cross-community developmental differences are attributed to differences in naming practices and belief systems in each community (Anggoro, Waxman, and Medin 2005; Waxman and Medin 2006).

Similarly, in a cross-cultural study of children from Israel, Japan, and the United States, children in all three countries were extremely accurate in attributing properties of living things to people, somewhat less accurate with other animals, and least accurate with plants. However, the study revealed culturally specific aspects of children's understanding of the term *alive.* Israeli children were considerably less likely to attribute to plants qualities that are shared by all living things. Japanese children, on the other hand, were more likely to attribute to inanimate entities (e.g., a rock) attributes that are unique to living things (Hatano and others 1993). These differences suggest that reasoning about a basic concept, such as life, is influenced by culture and linguistic factors. In the Israeli tradition, plants are regarded as different from humans and other animals. The Hebrew word for *animal,* but not for plants, is very close to that for *living* and *alive.* In contrast, Japanese culture includes a belief that plants are much like human beings, have feelings and emotions, and even inanimate entities are sometimes viewed as being alive. Parents may communicate such attitudes through actions and interactions with their children.

Preschool children understand that animals and plants grow and increase in size over time as they mature. Inanimate objects, such as toys and machines, may change in appearance due to wear and tear or the passing of time, but they do not change in size over time (Rosengren and others 1991; Hickling and Gelman 1995). Five-year-old children recognize that plants, but not objects, are similar to animals in terms of growing, needing food and/or water, and becoming older and dying (Inagaki and Hatano 1996). Three- and four-year-old children also realize that plants and animals may heal by themselves through regrowth (a rosebush will grow another rose; or a scratch on a finger will heal over time), but objects that are scratched or damaged (a shirt missing a button, or a car scratched on the side) must be repaired by human intervention (Backscheider, Shatz, and Gelman 1993). Overall, young preschool children can implicitly group living things together, particularly when asked about growth and other properties related to growth. However, it seems they are just beginning to have a consistent grasp of plants as biological entities. As noted by Carey (1985), young children can notice and learn about the properties of living things before they have a deeper understanding of the biological processes common to animals and plants.

Preschool children understand some aspects of growth in animals and plants. By three years of age, children realize that growth in animals involves an increase in size over time.

They realize that growth in animals is affected by food intake, not by an intention or desire to grow (Inagaki and Hatano 2002). Older children, approximately five years of age, also expect some animals to change in appearance with age. They understand that animals undergo metamorphosis—for example, caterpillars change into butterflies, and tadpoles change into frogs (Rosengren and others 1991). However, they realize that in natural transformations, such as growth or metamorphosis, the identity of animals remains constant despite changes in appearance with age (Gelman 2003).

Between the ages of four and five, children develop increasing knowledge about plants, including an understanding of some of the characteristics of plant growth and the nature of seeds (Hickling and Gelman 1995). Older four-year-olds realize that seeds originate from a natural source, specifically from same-species plants, not from other types of plants, and that people cannot make seeds. Older four-year-olds also expect external, natural mechanisms (sunshine and rain), rather than human activity or the intention and desire of the plant, to initiate the growth process. However, they have less understanding of what plants need, compared with animals, in order to grow. By around four and a half years of age, children also begin to appreciate the cyclical nature of plant growth. They recognize the predictable order of stages in plant growth from seed to plant, to flower and/or fruit, and back to seed.

Young children can identify body parts and processes (e.g., seeing, hearing, needing food, sleeping, breathing, falling ill) in humans and other animals. Knowledge about humans constitutes a useful and important base for young children, as they use it to infer knowledge about other animals and other living things (Carey 1985; Inagaki and Hatano 2002). According to this view, young children's familiarity with human body processes serves as a knowledge base to predict behaviors or attribute properties to unfamiliar animals and plants. The rationale is that knowledge about humans becomes useful in everyday biological problem solving and understanding, because humans share biological properties and processes with other living things. However, current research indicates that the role of humans in reasoning about other living things is shaped by experience, cultural beliefs, and practices. For example, a human-centered perspective is more common in children raised in urban environments, for whom direct experience with nature is relatively impoverished in comparison with rural children. Furthermore, culturally held belief systems of a given community also influence children's biological reasoning and the degree to which knowledge about humans is used in generalizing to other animals (Medin and others 2010).

Earth Sciences

Children have daily interactions with earth resources, including soil, rocks, and water, and become aware of natural changes in the earth such as the day-and-night cycle and climate changes associated with seasonal changes. Developmental research examined young children's reasoning about natural phenomena. Piaget argued that children tend to view humans as controlling all kinds of events in nature, attributing events and things on earth such as the construction of mountains, the clouds in the sky, and the existence of rivers and rocks to human control. However, contrary to Piaget's view, research indicates that children recognize that certain kinds of things are not under human control. In a study that asked children, "Do you think people make ____?," the question referred to either natural things such as the moon, clouds, dogs, salt (e.g., "Do you think people make the clouds?") or to objects used by humans, such as a cup or a car, preschool children tended to be highly accurate (Gelman 2003, 119). They recognize that natural things are not made by humans (Gelman and Kremer 1991).

Young children can observe and become aware of the earth's resources and phenomena, but they are not ready to grasp scientific concepts and explanations of the earth's phenomena such as the cause of the day/night cycle rotation or of seasonal changes (Kampeza 2006). Research on children's concepts of the earth is of great interest, particularly for educators who are concerned with how and when to introduce many topics related to earth and space. Several studies in the area of science education have shown that children acquire mature concepts about earth and gravity gradually, through distinct levels that go through seventh or eighth grade (Nussbaum and Novak 1976; Nussbaum 1979; Sneider and Pulos 1983). Initially, children (six to eight years of age) hold the view that the earth is flat and motionless. They may say that the earth is "round," but under more detailed questioning ("Where does the sun go at night?" "What does the earth look like when you look at it from very far away?"), they give answers consistent with the flat-earth view (Vosniadou and Brewer 1987, 58). Their concept of gravity is also still developing; so children who hold the view of a flat earth would argue that if there were people on the other side of the earth, they would fall off. Older children hold more advanced notions about the earth's shape and gravity. Children's concept of earth is being restructured, from a theory based on a flat, stationary earth to a theory based on a spherical rotating earth (Vosniadou and Brewer 1987). Cross-cultural studies of Mexican American, Native American, and Nepali children (Klein 1982; Diakidou, Vosnidau, and Hawks 1997; Mali and Howe 1979), and studies in Israel (Nussbaum 1979), and Greece (Kampeza 2006) found similar results. Mental representations of the earth held by children who live in different cultures may contain some elements from their particular culture (alternation of day and night is attributed to God), but all children start with similar mental representations of the earth.

A recent study of preschool children indicates that although most children can select the sphere as the earth's shape, they do not understand the relation between the earth's rotation and the day/night cycle (Kampeza 2006). Even after learning about the shapes of the sun and earth, as well as the cause of the day/night cycle, preschool children did not demonstrate an understanding of the day/night cycle. Subsequent to the learning session about earth, although the children accepted the earth as a spherical object, only a few children attributed the day/night cycle to the rotation of the earth on its axis (Valanides and

others 2000). Overall, research indicates that young children hold a concept of earth that conflicts with current scientific theories. Therefore, they cannot intuitively reason about the causes of everyday phenomena they observe, such as the day/night cycle, the seasons, and the apparent motion of the sun and the moon. However, daily interactions and experiences with earth resources and phenomena provide children with a foundation for future understanding of more abstract concepts in earth sciences.

Direct experiences with nature and earth materials and opportunities for direct contact with nature enhance children's connection to their natural environment and are likely to raise their awareness of issues related to care and protection of the environment (Musser and Diamond 1999; Paprotna 1998; Cohen and Horm-Wingerd 1993). Research indicates that during the preschool years children can become sensitive to basic ecological issues and can develop pro-environmental attitudes and behaviors. Studies that examined preschool children's ecological awareness found that young children seem to recognize the significance of issues associated with the environment. For example, preschool children can understand concepts such as recycling things, turning off water and light, picking up trash, not interfering with wild animals and plants, and caring for animals (Musser and Diamond 1999). Research indicates that preschool children can even become aware of ecological events and recognize the significance of environmental concerns such as the effects of water and air pollution, littering, overcrowding, and natural resource management, at a level commensurate

SCIENCE

with their existing knowledge (Cohen and Horm-Wingerd 1993). Furthermore, there is a positive relationship between young children's developing attitudes toward the environment and their parents' involvement of them in environmentally relevant activities. It is, therefore, reasonable to expect that ecologically sensitive practices in early childhood environments would be related to children's developing environmental attitudes and behaviors.

Glossary

animate/inanimate objects. Animate objects are living things with the capacity to initiate motion or activity. The term refers to animals (including humans) and is distinguished from inanimate objects, such as plants or nonliving objects (e.g., a car or a rock).

cause and effect. Cause is what makes something else happens (e.g., kicking the ball), and effect is what happens as a result of the cause (e.g., the ball is rolled).

classification. The sorting, grouping, or categorizing of objects according to established criteria.

communication. Refers to the skill of expressing ideas, describing observations, and discussing findings and explanations with others, either orally, through sign language, or in written form (drawings, charts, pictures, symbols).

compare and contrast. Looking at similarities and differences in real objects and events.

constructivist approach. An approach to learning in which children construct knowledge and build theories through active experimentation and interaction with objects and people in their environment rather than passively taking in information.

documentation. Preserving evidence by recording information, using different forms, including drawings, photographs, written transcripts, charts, journals, models, and constructions.

earth sciences. The study of the earth, includes topics related to properties of earth materials (soils, rocks, and minerals), the ocean, weather, and forces that shape the earth. Major components of earth sciences are geology and oceanography.

habitat. The home, place, or environment where an organism or a biological population normally lives.

homogeneous. Things of the same kind, with same form and property. In a homogenous substance, each component of the substance is the same.

hypothesis. A proposed explanation for an observable phenomena that can be tested by an experiment. A confirmed hypothesis supports a theory.

inference. Using logic to make an assumption or draw a conclusion that is based on observations but cannot be directly observed.

investigation. In the process of scientific inquiry, asking a question and conducting systematic observations or simple experiments to find an answer.

life cycle. The series of changes in the growth and development of humans, animals, or plants.

life sciences. The study of living things, including plants and animals, their characteristics, life cycles, habitats, and their interrelationships with each other and the environment. The three major branches of life sciences are biology, physiology, and ecology.

living things. Living organisms have the capacity for self-sustaining biological processes such as growth, breathing, reproduction, and responsiveness to stimuli. Examples of living things are humans, animals, and plants.

measurement tools. Simple tools, such as rulers, measuring cups and spoons, and scales, to measure length, volume, or weight.

observation. Gathering information about objects and events by using the senses of sight, smell, sound, touch, and taste and noticing specific details or phenomena that ordinarily might be overlooked.

observation tools. Tools to extend observations such as hand lenses, magnifying glasses, and binoculars.

physical properties. Observable features of a material, such as how it looks (e.g., shape, color), feels (e.g., solid, liquid, texture), or behaves (e.g., sinks in water).

physical sciences. The study of nonliving matter and energy. It deals with physical properties and transformations of substances, the nature of motion, force and energy (e.g., mechanical energy, heat, sound, light, electricity). The two major branches of physical sciences are physics and chemistry.

prediction. A guess or estimation that is based on prior observations, knowledge, and experiences.

predisposition. A tendency or inclination for something. In the context of early childhood science, young children have the predisposition, the inclination, and capacity to learn abstract concepts from biology and physics.

record. To set down information or knowledge in writing, drawings, or other permanent forms for the purpose of preserving evidence or tracking data over time.

scientific inquiry. Refers to the diverse ways in which scientists explore and develop knowledge and understanding of scientific ideas: making observations, posing questions, planning investigations, using tools to gather information, making predictions, recording information, and communicating findings and explanations.

substance. Any material with a definite chemical composition (e.g., water, salt, sugar, gold).

References and Source Materials

American Association for the Advancement of Science. 1993. *Benchmarks for Science Literacy: Project 2061.* New York: Oxford University Press.

———. 1999. *Dialogue on Early Childhood Science, Mathematics, and Technology Education.* Washington, DC: American Association for the Advancement of Science.

Anggoro, F. K., S. R. Waxman, and S. R. Medin. 2005. "The Effects of Naming Practices on Children's Understanding of Living Things." In *Proceedings of the Twenty-Seventh Annual Meeting of the Cognitive Science Society.* Edited by B. Bara, L. Barsalou, and M. Bucciarelli. Mahwah, NJ: Lawrence Erlbaum Associates.

Anglin, J. M. 1993. "Vocabulary Development: A Morphological Analysis." *Monographs of the Society for Research in Child Development* 58 (10), Serial No. 238: 1–166.

Au, T. K. August 1994. "Developing an Intuitive Understanding of Substance Kinds," *Cognitive Psychology* 27 (1): 71–111.

Backscheider, A. G., M. Shatz, and S. A. Gelman. 1993. "Preschoolers' Ability to Distinguish Living Kinds as a Function of Regrowth." *Child Development* 64:1242–57.

Baillargeon, R. 1995. "Physical Reasoning in Infancy." In *The Cognitive Neurosciences*, edited by M. S. Gazzaniga. Cambridge, MA: The MIT Press.

Baillargeon, R., A. Needham, and J. DeVos. 1992. "The Development of Young Infants' Intuitions about Support." *Early Development and Parenting* 1 (2): 69–78.

Bellanca, J., and R. Brandt, eds. 2010. *21st Century Skills: Rethinking How Students Learn.* Bloomington, IN: Solution Tree.

Brenneman, K., J. Stevenson-Boyd, and E. C. Frede. 2009. *Math and Science in Preschool: Policies and Practice.* Preschool Policy Brief, Issue No. 19. New Brunswick, NJ: National Institute for Early Education Research.

Brown, A. L. 1990. "Domain-Specific Principles Affect Learning and Transfer in Children." *Cognitive Science* 14:107–33.

Bullock, M., R. Gelman, and R. Baillargeon. 1982. "The Development of Causal Reasoning." In *The Developmental Psychology of Time*, edited by W. J. Friedman. New York: Academic Press.

California Department of Education. 2008. *California Preschool Learning Foundations, Volume 1.* Sacramento: California Department of Education.

Carey, S. 1985. *Conceptual Change in Childhood.* Cambridge, MA: MIT Press.

Carey, S., and R. Gelman, eds. *The Epigenesis of Mind: Essays on Biology and Cognition.* 1991. Hillsdale, NJ: Lawrence Erlbaum Associates.

Chaille, C., and L. Britain. 2002. *The Young Child as Scientist: A Constructivist Approach to Early Childhood Science Education*, 3rd ed. Boston, MA: Allyn and Bacon.

Cohen, S., and D. Horm-Wingerd. 1993. "Children and the Environment: Ecological Awareness Among Preschool Children." *Environment and Behavior* 25 (1): 103–20.

Conezio, K., and L. French. September 2002. "Science in the Preschool Classroom: Capitalizing on Children's Fascination with the Everyday World to Foster Language and Literacy Development." *Young Children* 57:12–18.

DeVries, R., and others. 2002. *Developing Constructivist Early Childhood Curriculum: Practical Principles and Activities.* New York: Teachers College Press.

Diakidoy, I. A., S. Vosniadou, and J. D. Hawks. 1997. "Conceptual Change in Astronomy: Models of the Earth and of the Day/Night Cycle in American-Indian Children." *European Journal of Psychology of Education* 12 (2): 159–84.

Dunbar, K., and D. Klahr. 1989. "Developmental Differences in Scientific Discovery Strategies." In *Complex Information Processing: The Impact of Herbert A. Simon,* edited by D. Klahr and K. Kotovsky. Hillsdale, NJ: Lawrence Erlbaum Associates.

Eshach, H. 2006. *Science Literacy in Primary Schools and Pre-Schools.* Dordrecht, The Netherlands: Springer.

French, L. 2004. "Science as the Center of a Coherent, Integrated Early Childhood Curriculum." *Early Childhood Research Quarterly* 19 (1): 138–49.

Gelman, R. 1990. "First Principles Organize Attention to and Learning About Relevant Data: Number and the Animate-Inanimate Distinction as Examples." *Cognitive Science* 14 (1): 79–106.

Gelman, R., and R. Baillargeon. 1983. "A Review of Some Piagetian Concepts." In Vol. III of *Handbook of Child Psychology: Cognitive Development,* edited by J. H. Flavell and E. M. Markman. New York: Wiley.

Gelman, R., and K. Brenneman. 2004. "Science Learning Pathways for Young Children." *Early Childhood Quarterly Review* 19:150–58.

Gelman, R., and others. 2010. *Preschool Pathways to Science: Facilitating Scientific Ways of Thinking, Talking, Doing, and Understanding.* Baltimore, MD: Paul H. Brookes Publishing.

Gelman, R., E. S. Spelke, and E. Meck. 1983. "What Preschoolers Know About Animate and Inanimate Objects." In *The Acquisition of Symbolic Skills,* edited by D. Rogers and J. A. Sloboda. London: Plenum.

Gelman, S. A. 2003. *The Essential Child: Origins of Essentialism in Everyday Thought.* London: Oxford University Press.

Gelman, S. A., and K. E., Kremer. 1991. "Understanding Natural Cause: Children's Explanations of How Objects and Their Properties Originate." *Child Development* 62 (2): 396–414.

Gelman, S. A., and E. M. Markman. 1986. "Categories and Induction in Young Children." *Cognition* 23:183–209.

———. 1987. "Young Children's Inductions from Natural Kinds: The Role of Categories and Appearances." *Child Development* 58:1532–41.

Gelman, S. A., and H. M., Wellman. 1991. "Insides and Essences: Early Understandings of the Non-obvious." *Cognition* 38:213–44.

Gopnik, A., and others. 2001. "Causal Learning Mechanisms in Very Young Children: Two-, Three- and Four-Year-Olds Infer Causal Relations from Patterns of Variation and Covariation." *Developmental Psychology* 37 (5): 620–29.

Hatano, G., and others. 1993. "The Development of Biological Knowledge: A Multi-National Study." *Cognitive Development* 8 (1): 47–62.

Hickling, A. K., and S. A., Gelman. 1995. "How Does Your Garden Grow? Evidence of Early Conception of Plants as Biological Kinds." *Child Development* 66 (3): 856–76.

Inagaki, K. 1990. "The Effects of Raising Animals on Children's Biological Knowledge." *British Journal of Developmental Psychology* 8 (2): 119–29.

Inagaki, K., and G. Hatano. 1996. "Young Children's Recognition of Commonalities Between Animals and Plants." *Child Development* 67 (6): 2823–40.

———. 2002. *Young Children's Naïve Thinking About the Biological World.* New York: Psychology Press.

Inhelder, B., and J. Piaget. 1958. *The Growth of Logical Thinking from Childhood to Adolescence.* Translated by A. Parsons and S. Milgram. New York: Basic Books.

SCIENCE

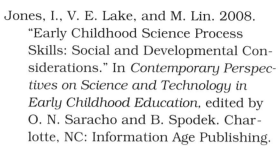

SCIENCE

Jones, I., V. E. Lake, and M. Lin. 2008. "Early Childhood Science Process Skills: Social and Developmental Considerations." In *Contemporary Perspectives on Science and Technology in Early Childhood Education*, edited by O. N. Saracho and B. Spodek. Charlotte, NC: Information Age Publishing.

Kamii, C., and R. DeVries. 1993. *Physical Knowledge in Preschool Education: Implications of Piaget's Theory*. New York: Teachers College Press.

Kampeza, M. 2006. "Preschool Children's Ideas about the Earth as a Cosmic Body and the Day/Night Cycle." *Journal of Science Education* 7 (2): 119–22.

Keil, F. C. 1989. *Concepts, Kinds, and Cognitive Development*. Cambridge, MA: MIT Press.

Klein, C. A. 1982. "Children's Concepts of the Earth and the Sun: A Cross Cultural Study." *Science Education* 66 (1): 95–107.

Kellert, S. R. 2002. "Experiencing Nature: Affective, Cognitive, and Evaluative Development in Children." In *Children and Nature: Psychological, Sociocultural and Evolutionary Investigations*, edited by P. H. Kahn and S. R. Kellert. Cambridge: The MIT Press.

Leslie, A. M. 1994. "ToMM, ToBy, and Agency: Core Architecture and Domain Specificity." In *Mapping the Mind: Domain Specificity in Cognition and Culture*, edited by L. A. Hirschfeld and S. A. Gelman. New York: Cambridge University Press.

Leslie, A. M., and S. Keeble. 1987. "Do Six-Month-Old Infants Perceive Causality?" *Cognition* 25 (3): 265–88.

Lind, K. K. 1997. "Science in the Developmentally Appropriate Integrated Curriculum." In *Integrated Curriculum and Developmentally Appropriate Practice: Birth to Age Eight*, edited by C. H. Hart, D. C. Burts, and R. Charlesworth. Albany, NY: State University of New York Press.

———. 1999. "Science in Early Childhood: Developing and Acquiring Fundamental Concepts and Skills." In *Dialogue on Early Childhood Science, Mathematics, and Technology Education*. Washington, DC: American Association for the Advancement of Science.

———. 2005. *Exploring Science in Early Childhood Education*. 4th ed. Clifton Park, NY: Delmar Cengage Learning.

Mali, G. B., and A. Howe. 1979. "Development of Earth and Gravity Concepts Among Nepali Children." *Science Education* 63 (5): 685–91.

Martin, D. J. 2001. *Constructing Early Childhood Science*. Albany, NY: Thomson Delmar Learning.

Massey, C. M., and R. Gelman. 1988. "Preschoolers' Ability to Decide Whether a Photographed Unfamiliar Object Can Move Itself." *Developmental Psychology* 24 (3): 307–17.

Medin, D., and others. 2010. "Human-Centeredness Is Not a Universal Feature of Young Children's Reasoning: Culture and Experience Matter When Reasoning about Biological Entities." *Cognitive Development* 25:197–207.

Metz, K. E. 1993. "Preschoolers' Developing Knowledge of the Pan Balance: From New Representation to Transformed Problem Solving." *Cognition and Instruction* 11 (1): 31–93.

Michaels, S., A. W. Shouse, and H. A. Schweingruber. 2008. *Ready, Set, Science! Putting Research to Work in K–8 Science Classrooms*. Washington, DC: The National Academies Press.

Musser, L. M., and K. E. Diamond. 1999. "The Children's Attitudes Toward the Environment Scale for Preschool Children." *The Journal of Environmental Education* 30 (2): 23–30.

National Committee on Science Education Standards and Assessment and National Research Council. 1996. *National Science Education Standards*. Center for Science, Mathematics and

Engineering Education. Washington, DC: National Academies Press.

National Research Council. 1999. *How People Learn: Brain, Mind, Experience, and School.* Edited by the Committee on Developments in the Science of Learning, J. D. Bransford, A. L. Brown, and R. R. Cooking. Commission on Behavioral and Social Sciences and Education. Washington, DC: National Academies Press.

———. 2000. *Eager to Learn: Educating Our Preschoolers.* Edited by the Committee on Early Childhood Pedagogy, B. T. Bowman, M. S. Donovan, and M. S. Burns. Commission on Behavioral and Social Sciences and Education. Washington, DC: National Academies Press.

———. 2007. *Taking Science to School: Learning and Teaching Science in Grades K–8.* Edited by the Committee on Science Learning, Kindergarten through Eighth Grade, R. A. Duschl, H. A. Schweingruber, and A. W. Shouse. Board on Science Education, Center for Education. Division of Social Sciences and Education. Washington, DC: The National Academies Press.

Nguyen, S. P., and S. A. Gelman. 2002. "Four- and Six-Year-Olds' Biological Concept of Death: The Case of Plants." *British Journal of Developmental Psychology* 20 (4): 495–513.

Nussbaum, J. 1979. "Children's Conceptions of the Earth as a Cosmic Body: A Cross Age Study." *Science Education* 63 (1): 83–93.

Nussbaum, J., and J. D. Novak. 1976. "An Assessment of Children's Concepts of the Earth Utilizing Structured Interviews." *Science Education* 60 (4): 535–50.

Oakes, L. M., and L. B. Cohen. 1990. "Infant Perception of a Causal Event." *Cognitive Development* 5 (2): 193–207.

Paprotna, G. 1998. "On the Understanding of Ecological Concepts by Children of Pre-School Age." *International Journal of Early Years Education* 6 (2): 155–64.

Peterson, S. M., and L. French. 2008. "Supporting Young Children's Explanations Through Inquiry Science in Preschool." *Early Childhood Research Quarterly* 23 (3): 395–408.

Piaget, J. 1952. *The Origins of Intelligence in Children.* Translated by M. Cook. New York: International Universities Press.

Prasada, S. 1993. "Learning Names for Solid Substances: Quantifying Solid Entities in Terms of Portions." *Cognitive Development* 8 (1): 83–104.

Richards, D. D., and R. S. Siegler. 1986. "Children's Understandings of the Attributes of Life." *Journal of Experimental Child Psychology* 42 (1): 1–22.

Rosengren, K. S., and others. 1991. "As Time Goes By: Children's Early Understanding of Biological Growth in Animals." *Child Development* 62 (6): 1302–20.

Ruffman, T., and others. 1993. "Reflecting on Scientific Thinking: Children's Understanding of the Hypothesis–Evidence Relation." *Child Development* 64 (6): 1617–36.

Russell, T., W. Harlen, and D. Watt. 1989. "Children's Ideas About Evaporation." *International Journal of Science Education* 11 (5): 566–76.

Schauble, L. 1990. "Belief Revision in Children: The Role of Prior Knowledge and Strategies for Generating Evidence." *Journal of Experimental Child Psychology* 49 (1): 31–57.

Schulz, L. E., and E. B. Bonawitz. 2007. "Serious Fun: Preschoolers Engage in More Exploratory Play When Evidence Is Confounded." *Developmental Psychology* 43 (4): 1045–50.

Schulz, L. E., E. B. Bonawitz, and T. L. Griffiths. 2007. "Can Being Scared Cause Tummy Aches? Naïve Theories, Ambiguous Evidence, and Preschoolers' Causal Inferences." *Developmental Psychology* 43 (5): 1124–39.

Schulz, L. E., and A. Gopnik. 2004. "Causal Learning Across Domains."

Developmental Psychology 40 (2): 162–76.

Smith, C., S. Carey, and M. Wiser. 1985. "On Differentiation: A Case Study of the Development of the Concepts of Size, Weight, and Density." *Cognition* 21 (3): 177–237.

Sneider, C., and S. Pulos. 1983. "Children's Cosmographies: Understanding the Earth's Shape and Gravity." *Science Education* 67 (2): 205–21.

Sodian, B., D. Zaitchik, and S. Carey. 1991. "Young Children's Differentiation of Hypothetical Beliefs from Evidence." *Child Development* 62 (4): 753–66.

Soja, N. N., S. Carey, and E. S. Spelke. 1991. "Ontological Categories Guide Young Children's Inductions of Word Meaning: Object Terms and Substance Terms." *Cognition* 38 (2): 179–211.

Spelke, E. S. 1990. "Principles of Object Perception." *Cognitive Science* 14: 29–56.

Spelke, E. S., and others. 1992. "Origins of Knowledge." *Psychological Review* 99 (4): 605–32.

Subrahmanyam, K., R. Gelman, and A. Lafosse. 2002. "Animate and Other Separably Moveable Objects." In *Category-Specificity in Brain and Mind*, edited by E. Fordes and G. Humphreys. London, England: Psychology Press.

Valanides, N., and others. 2000. "Changing Pre-school Children's Conceptions of the Day/Night Cycle." *International Journal of Early Years Education* 8 (1): 27–39.

Vosniadou, S., and W. F. Brewer. 1987. "Theories of Knowledge Restructuring in Development." *Review of Educational Research* 57 (1): 51–67.

Waxman, S. R., and D. L. Medin. 2006. "Core Knowledge, Naming and the Acquisition of the Fundamental (Folk) biologic Concept 'Alive'." In *Proceedings of the Fifth International Conference of the Cognitive Science*, edited by N. Miyake. Mahwah, NJ: Lawrence Erlbaum.

Waxman, S. R., and D. Medin. 2007. "Experience and Cultural Models Matter: Placing Firm Limits on Anthropocentrism." *Human Development* 50 (1): 23–30.

Waxman, S. R., D. L. Medin, and N. Ross. 2007. "Folkbiological Reasoning from a Cross-cultural Developmental Perspective: Early Essentialist Notions are Shaped by Cultural Beliefs." *Developmental Psychology* 43 (2): 294–308.

Worth, K., and S. Grollman. 2003. *Worms, Shadows, and Whirlpools: Science in the Early Childhood Classroom*. Portsmouth, NH: Heinemann.

Zur, O., and R. Gelman. 2004. "Young Children Can Add and Subtract by Predicting and Checking." *Early Childhood Research Quarterly* 19 (1): 121–37.

SCIENCE

APPENDIX A

The Foundations

History–Social Science

Self and Society

1.0 Culture and Diversity

At around 48 months of age	*At around 60 months of age*
1.1 Exhibit developing cultural, ethnic, and racial identity and understand relevant language and cultural practices. Display curiosity about diversity in human characteristics and practices, but prefer those of their own group.	1.1 Manifest stronger cultural, ethnic, and racial identity and greater familiarity with relevant language, traditions, and other practices. Show more interest in human diversity, but strongly favor characteristics of their own group.

2.0 Relationships

2.1 Interact comfortably with many peers and adults; actively contribute to creating and maintaining relationships with a few significant adults and peers.	2.1 Understand the mutual responsibilities of relationships; take initiative in developing relationships that are mutual, cooperative, and exclusive.

3.0 Social Roles and Occupations

3.1 Play familiar adult social roles and occupations (such as parent, teacher, and doctor) consistent with their developing knowledge of these roles.	3.1 Exhibit more sophisticated understanding of a broader variety of adult roles and occupations, but uncertain how work relates to income.

Becoming a Preschool Community Member (Civics)

1.0 Skills for Democratic Participation

At around 48 months of age	At around 60 months of age
1.1 Identify as members of a group, participate willingly in group activities, and begin to understand and accept responsibility as group members, although assistance is required in coordinating personal interests with those of others.	1.1 Become involved as responsible participants in group activities, with growing understanding of the importance of considering others' opinions, group decision making, and respect for majority rules and the views of group members who disagree with the majority.

2.0 Responsible Conduct

2.1 Strive to cooperate with group expectations to maintain adult approval and get along with others. Self-control is inconsistent, however, especially when children are frustrated or upset.	2.1 Exhibit responsible conduct more reliably as children develop self-esteem (and adult approval) from being responsible group members. May also manage others' behavior to ensure that others also fit in with group expectations.

3.0 Fairness and Respect for Other People

3.1 Respond to the feelings and needs of others with simple forms of assistance, sharing, and turn-taking. Understand the importance of rules that protect fairness and maintain order.	3.1 Pay attention to others' feelings, more likely to provide assistance, and try to coordinate personal desires with those of other children in mutually satisfactory ways. Actively support rules that protect fairness to others.

4.0 Conflict Resolution

4.1 Can use simple bargaining strategies and seek adult assistance when in conflict with other children or adults, although frustration, distress, or aggression also occurs.	4.1 More capable of negotiating, compromising, and finding cooperative means of resolving conflict with peers or adults, although verbal aggression may also result.

Sense of Time
(History)

1.0 Understanding Past Events

At around 48 months of age	At around 60 months of age
1.1 Recall past experiences easily and enjoy hearing stories about the past, but require adult help to determine when past events occurred in relation to each other and to connect them with current experience.	1.1 Show improving ability to relate past events to other past events and current experiences, although adult assistance continues to be important.

2.0 Anticipating and Planning Future Events

2.1 Anticipate events in familiar situations in the near future, with adult assistance.	2.1 Distinguish when future events will happen, plan for them, and make choices (with adult assistance) that anticipate future needs.

3.0 Personal History

3.1 Proudly display developing skills to attract adult attention and share simple accounts about recent experiences.	3.1 Compare current abilities with skills at a younger age and share more detailed autobiographical stories about recent experiences.

4.0 Historical Changes in People and the World

4.1 Easily distinguish older family members from younger ones (and other people) and events in the recent past from those that happened "long ago," although do not readily sequence historical events on a timeline.	4.1 Develop an interest in family history (e.g., when family members were children) as well as events of "long ago," and begin to understand when these events occurred in relation to each other.

Sense of Place
(Geography and Ecology)

1.0 Navigating Familiar Locations

At around 48 months of age	*At around 60 months of age*
1.1 Identify the characteristics of familiar locations such as home and school, describe objects and activities associated with each, recognize the routes between them, and begin using simple directional language (with various degrees of accuracy).	1.1 Comprehend larger familiar locations, such as the characteristics of their community and region (including hills and streams, weather, common activities) and the distances between familiar locations (such as between home and school), and compare their home community with those of others.

2.0 Caring for the Natural World

2.1 Show an interest in nature (including animals, plants, and weather) especially as children have direct experience with them. Begin to understand human interactions with the environment (such as pollution in a lake or stream) and the importance of taking care of plants and animals.	2.1 Show an interest in a wider range of natural phenomena, including those not directly experienced (such as snow for a child living in Southern California), and are more concerned about caring for the natural world and the positive and negative impacts of people on the natural world (e.g., recycling, putting trash in trash cans).

3.0 Understanding the Physical World Through Drawings and Maps

3.1 Can use drawings, globes, and maps to refer to the physical world, although often unclear on the use of map symbols.	3.1 Create their own drawings, maps, and models; are more skilled at using globes, maps, and map symbols; and use maps for basic problem solving (such as locating objects) with adult guidance.

Marketplace (Economics)

1.0 Exchange

At around 48 months of age	At around 60 months of age
1.1 Understand ownership, limited supply, what stores do, give-and-take, and payment of money to sellers. Show interest in money and its function, but still figuring out the relative value of coins.	1.1 Understand more complex economic concepts (e.g., bartering; more money is needed for things of greater value; if more people want something, more will be sold).

Science

Scientific Inquiry

1.0 Observation and Investigation

At around 48 months of age	*At around 60 months of age*
1.1 Demonstrate curiosity and raise simple questions about objects and events in their environment.	1.1 Demonstrate curiosity and an increased ability to raise questions about objects and events in their environment.
1.2 Observe[1] objects and events in the environment and describe them.	1.2 Observe objects and events in the environment and describe them in greater detail.
1.3 Begin to identify and use, with adult support, some observation and measurement tools.	1.3 Identify and use a greater variety of observation and measurement tools. May spontaneously use an appropriate tool, though may still need adult support.
1.4 Compare and contrast objects and events and begin to describe similarities and differences.	1.4 Compare and contrast objects and events and describe similarities and differences in greater detail.
1.5 Make predictions and check them, with adult support, through concrete experiences.	1.5 Demonstrate an increased ability to make predictions and check them (e.g., may make more complex predictions, offer ways to test predictions, and discuss why predictions were correct or incorrect).
1.6 Make inferences and form generalizations based on evidence.	1.6 Demonstrate an increased ability to make inferences and form generalizations based on evidence.

1. Other related scientific processes, such as classifying, ordering, and measuring, are addressed in the foundations for mathematics.

2.0 Documentation and Communication

At around 48 months of age	*At around 60 months of age*
2.1 Record observations or findings in various ways, with adult assistance, including pictures, words (dictated to adults), charts, journals, models, and photos.	2.1 Record information more regularly and in greater detail in various ways, with adult assistance, including pictures, words (dictated to adults), charts, journals, models, photos, or by tallying and graphing information.
2.2 Share findings and explanations, which may be correct or incorrect, with or without adult prompting.	2.2 Share findings and explanations, which may be correct or incorrect, more spontaneously and with greater detail.

Physical Sciences

1.0 Properties and Characteristics of Nonliving Objects and Materials

At around 48 months of age	*At around 60 months of age*
1.1 Observe, investigate, and identify the characteristics and physical properties of objects and of solid and nonsolid materials (size, weight, shape, color, texture, and sound).	1.1 Demonstrate increased ability to observe, investigate, and describe in greater detail the characteristics and physical properties of objects and of solid and nonsolid materials (size, weight, shape, color, texture, and sound).

2.0 Changes in Nonliving Objects and Materials

2.1 Demonstrate awareness that objects and materials can change; explore and describe changes in objects and materials (rearrangement of parts; change in color, shape, texture, temperature).	2.1 Demonstrate an increased awareness that objects and materials can change in various ways. Explore and describe in greater detail changes in objects and materials (rearrangement of parts; change in color, shape, texture, form, and temperature).

2.0 Changes in Nonliving Objects and Materials *(continued)*

At around 48 months of age	*At around 60 months of age*
2.2 Observe and describe the motion of objects (in terms of speed, direction, the ways things move), and explore the effect of own actions (e.g., pushing pulling, rolling, dropping) on making objects move.	2.2 Demonstrate an increased ability to observe and describe in greater detail the motion of objects (in terms of speed, direction, the ways things move), and to explore the effect of own actions on the motion of objects, including changes in speed and direction.

Life Sciences

1.0 Properties and Characteristics of Living Things

At around 48 months of age	*At around 60 months of age*
1.1 Identify characteristics of a variety of animals and plants, including appearance (inside and outside) and behavior, and begin to categorize them.	1.1 Identify characteristics of a greater variety of animals and plants and demonstrate an increased ability to categorize them.
1.2 Begin to indicate knowledge of body parts and processes (e.g., eating, sleeping, breathing, walking) in humans and other animals.[2]	1.2 Indicate greater knowledge of body parts and processes (e.g., eating, sleeping, breathing, walking) in humans and other animals.
1.3 Identify the habitats of people and familiar animals and plants in the environment and begin to realize that living things have habitats in different environments.	1.3 Recognize that living things have habitats in different environments suited to their unique needs.
1.4 Indicate knowledge of the difference between animate objects (animals, people) and inanimate objects. For example, expect animate objects to initiate movement and to have different insides than inanimate objects.	1.4 Indicate knowledge of the difference between animate and inanimate objects, providing greater detail, and recognize that only animals and plants undergo biological processes such as growth, illness, healing, and dying.

2. The knowledge of body parts is also addressed in the *California Preschool Foundations (Volume 2)* for health. In science, it also includes the knowledge of body processes. Knowledge of body parts is extended to those of humans and other animals.

2.0 Changes in Living Things

At around 48 months of age	At around 60 months of age
2.1 Observe and explore growth and changes in humans, animals, and plants and demonstrate an understanding that living things change over time in size and in other capacities as they grow.	2.1 Observe and explore growth in humans, animals, and plants and demonstrate an increased understanding that living things change as they grow and go through transformations related to the life cycle (for example, from a caterpillar to butterfly).
2.2 Recognize that animals and plants require care and begin to associate feeding and watering with the growth of humans, animals, and plants.	2.2 Develop a greater understanding of the basic needs of humans, animals, and plants (e.g., food, water, sunshine, shelter).

Earth Sciences

1.0 Properties and Characteristics of Earth Materials and Objects

At around 48 months of age	At around 60 months of age
1.1 Investigate characteristics (size, weight, shape, color, texture) of earth materials such as sand, rocks, soil, water, and air.	1.1 Demonstrate increased ability to investigate and compare characteristics (size, weight, shape, color, texture) of earth materials such as sand, rocks, soil, water, and air.

2.0 Changes in the Earth

2.1 Observe and describe natural objects in the sky (sun, moon, stars, clouds) and how they appear to move and change.	2.1 Demonstrate an increased ability to observe and describe natural objects in the sky and to notice patterns of movement and apparent changes in the sun and the moon.
2.2 Notice and describe changes in weather.	2.2 Demonstrate an increased ability to observe, describe, and discuss changes in weather.
2.3 Begin to notice the effects of weather and seasonal changes on their own lives and on plants and animals.	2.3 Demonstrate an increased ability to notice and describe the effects of weather and seasonal changes on their own lives and on plants and animals.
2.4 Develop awareness of the importance of caring for and respecting the environment and participate in activities related to its care.	2.4 Demonstrate an increased awareness and the ability to discuss in simple terms how to care for the environment, and participate in activities related to its care.

APPENDIX B

The Foundations

An Overview of the Alignment of the California Preschool Learning Foundations with Key Early Education Resources

Introduction

Over the past 15 years, the California Department of Education (CDE) has identified foundations to describe the learning and development of children from birth through kindergarten. This work focused on what young children know and are able to do during different age periods. Work on the period covering birth through kindergarten stemmed from three distinct initiatives. First, academic content experts, K–12 educators, and other stakeholders collaborated to define what children are expected to learn in California public schools from kindergarten through twelfth grade. Standards in eight domains emerged from this effort. There are standards for the following subjects in K–12 education: English language arts, English-language development, mathematics, visual and performing arts, physical education, health education, history–social science, school library, and science.

In 2006, experts were convened to write foundations that describe the learning and development of children during the years from birth to age three. The publication *California Infant/Toddler Learning and Development Foundations* represents the second step in the CDE's work. Experts recommended that the term *foundations* be used rather than *standards,* because early learning and development reflects a developmental process that lays the foundation for academic learning at school age. The infant/toddler learning and development foundations are organized into four domains:

- Social–Emotional Development
- Language Development
- Cognitive Development
- Perceptual and Motor Development

After creating the infant/toddler learning and development foundations, the CDE proceeded with the third step. Researchers, early childhood educators, and other stakeholders convened to conceptualize and delineate preschool learning foundations. This effort produced learning foundations that cover nine developmental domains: Social-Emotional Development, Language and Literacy, English-Language Development, and Mathematics (Volume 1); Visual and Performing Arts, Physical Development, and Health (Volume 2); and History-Social Science and Science (Volume 3).

As work on standards and foundations continues to evolve in California, two national initiatives have contributed to early childhood educators' understanding of learning and development: (1) the Common Core State Standards (CCSS) and (2) the *Head Start Child Development and Early Learning Framework (Head Start Learning Framework)*. The CCSS provide standards for every grade level from kindergarten through twelfth grade for English Language Arts and Literacy in History/Social Studies, Science, and Technical Subjects; and for Mathematics. California stands among numerous states that have adopted the CCSS. The *Head Start Learning Framework* describes key learning in 11 developmental domains: Physical Development & Health, Social & Emotional Development, Approaches to Learning, Logic & Reasoning, Language Development, English Language Development, Literacy Knowledge & Skills, Mathematics Knowledge & Skills, Science Knowledge & Skills, Creative Arts Expression, and Social Studies Knowledge & Skills. Head Start programs throughout the country orient the support of young children's development and learning around the knowledge and skills described in the Framework.

These resources share the purpose of promoting the intentional support of young children's learning and development. By focusing on the key knowledge and skills that children progressively acquire during the first years of life, early childhood educators can develop curriculum that is in tune with early learning. In particular, they can be attentive to significant learning, document it, and reflectively plan how to facilitate it. Additional resources that work hand in hand with standards and foundations have been created for early childhood educators. For example, the CDE's infant/toddler curriculum framework is aligned with the infant/toddler learning and development foundations, and the preschool curriculum framework is aligned with the preschool learning foundations. The Desired Results Developmental Profile is also aligned with the infant/toddler and preschool foundations.

An important question is, How do the preschool learning foundations align with the infant/toddler learning and development foundations, the kindergarten content standards, the CCSS, and the *Head Start Learning Framework?*

The following table presents an alignment of the domains across the infant/toddler learning and development foundations, the preschool learning foundations, and the kindergarten content standards, the CCSS, and the *Head Start Learning Framework.*

Table 1

Overview Alignment of the Domains in the California Preschool Learning Foundations with Domains in Key Early Education Resources

Domains					
California Preschool Learning Foundations	**California Infant/ Toddler Learning and Development Foundations**	**California Kindergarten Content Standards**	**Common Core State Standards**	**Head Start Child Development and Early Learning Framework**	**Additional Domains in the Head Start Child Development and Early Learning Framework with Corresponding Content**
Social–Emotional Development	Social–Emotional Development	Health Education Mental, Emotional, and Social Health		Social & Emotional Development	Approaches to Learning Logic & Reasoning
Language and Literacy	Language Development	English–Language Arts	English–Language Arts	Language Development Literacy Knowledge & Skills	
English– Language Development	Language Development	English–Language Development		English Language Development	Literacy Knowledge & Skills
Mathematics	Cognitive Development	Mathematics	Mathematics	Mathematics Knowledge & Skills	Logic & Reasoning Approaches to Learning
Visual and Performing Arts	All Domains	Visual and Performing Arts		Creative Arts Expression	Logic & Reasoning
Physical Development	Perceptual and Motor Development Cognitive Development	Physical Education		Physical Development & Health	
Health	All Domains	Health Education		Physical Development & Health	
History–Social Science	Social–Emotional Development Cognitive Development	History–Social Science		Social Studies Knowledge & Skills	Social & Emotional Development
Science	Cognitive Development Language Development	Science		Science Knowledge & Skills	Approaches to Learning Logic & Reasoning

As the Overview table indicates, the developmental domains at the infant/toddler level (e.g., Social–Emotional, Language, Cognitive, and Perceptual and Motor Development) align with corresponding preschool domains. The foundations in the Social–Emotional Development domain at the infant/toddler level are aligned with the Social–Emotional Development foundations at the preschool level. The Language Development domain at the infant/toddler level aligns with the Language and Literacy domain at the preschool level. The infant/toddler foundations for Language Development also align with foundations for English-Language Development at the preschool level. The domain of Cognitive Development covers a broad range of knowledge and skills at the infant/toddler level. Some of the cognitive competencies align with foundations in the Mathematics domain at the preschool level. Additionally, some cognitive competencies align with foundations in the preschool domains of Physical Development, History–Social Science, and Science. All infant/toddler domains have content that pertains, in one way or another, to the Visual and Performing Arts domain at the preschool level. The Perceptual and Motor Development domain and some components from Cognitive Development at the infant/toddler level align with the Physical Development domain at the preschool level. Finally, all domains of the infant/toddler foundations are related to the Health foundations for preschool children.

The domains of the preschool learning foundations directly correspond to the domains of California's kindergarten content standards. As the Overview table shows, the content of the Social–Emotional Development domain at the preschool level overlaps with content in the Mental, Emotional, and Social Health strand of the Health domain at kindergarten age. The remaining domains line up in a straightforward manner across age levels: The preschool Language and Literacy domain aligns with the kindergarten English-Language Arts domain; the preschool Mathematics domain with the kindergarten Mathematics domain; the preschool Visual and Performing Arts domain with the kindergarten Visual and Performing Arts domain; the

preschool Physical Development domain with the kindergarten Physical Education domain; the preschool Health domain with the kindergarten Health Education domain; the preschool History-Social Science domain with the kindergarten History-Social Science domain; and the preschool Science domain with the kindergarten Science domain.

In addition to the one-to-one correspondence between the domains of the preschool learning foundations and those of the kindergarten content standards, the preschool Language and Literacy domain aligns with the CCSS English language arts domain. Likewise, the preschool Mathematics domain aligns with the CCSS Mathematics domain.

The alignment between the preschool learning foundations and the *Head Start Learning Framework* consists of two parts. First, for each of the preschool learning foundations domains, the *Head Start Learning Framework* has content in a corresponding domain (in one case, two domains). Thus, the preschool learning foundations' Social–Emotional Development domain aligns with the *Head Start Learning Framework*'s Social & Emotional Development domain, the preschool Language and Literacy domain with Head Start's Language Development and Literacy Knowledge & Skills domains, the preschool English-Language Development domain with Head Start's English Language Development domain, the preschool Mathematics domain with Head Start's Mathematics Knowledge & Skills domain, the preschool Visual and Performing Arts domain with Head Start's Creative Arts Expression domain, the preschool Physical Development domain with Head Start's Physical Development & Health domain, the preschool Health domain with Head Start's Physical Development & Health domain, the preschool History–Social Science domain with Head Start's Social Studies Knowledge & Skills domain, and the preschool Science domain with Head Start's Science Knowledge & Skills domain.

The second part of the alignment between the content of the *California Preschool Learning Foundations* and that of the *Head Start Learning Framework* centers on the cross-cutting nature of some of the domains in the latter document. The *Head Start Learning Framework*'s Approaches to Learning domain has content that relates to content in the Social–Emotional Development, Mathematics, and Science domains of the preschool learning foundations. Similarly, the content of the Head Start's Logic & Reasoning domain intersects with the preschool learning foundations' Social–Emotional Development, Mathematics, Visual and Performing Arts, and Science domains. Two other *Head Start Learning Framework* domains have content that pertains to additional preschool learning domains: Head Start's Literacy Knowledge & Skills aligns with parts of the preschool English-Language Development domain, and Head Start's Social Studies Knowledge & Skills aligns with a few foundations in the preschool Social–Emotional Development domain.

The following sections present an overview of the alignment of the preschool foundations with the infant/toddler foundations, the kindergarten content standards, the CCSS for kindergarten, and the Head Start Learning Framework. The detailed alignment document (http://www.cde.ca.gov/sp/cd/re/documents/reversealignment.pdf) provides summaries of the developmental progression of the preschool foundations in each domain as they relate to specific infant/toddler foundations, specific CCSS, specific kindergarten content standards, and specific competencies described in the *Head Start Learning Framework*.

Alignment of the California Infant/Toddler Learning and Development Foundations, Preschool Learning Foundations, and Kindergarten Content Standards for Each Domain

Social–Emotional Development

This section describes an overview of the alignment of the preschool foundations in social–emotional development with the infant/toddler learning and development foundations, and with the kindergarten content standards. Table 2 shows how the substrands of preschool learning foundations in social–emotional development align with the infant/toddler foundations in social–emotional development and with the kindergarten content standards in *mental, emotional, and social health*. A detailed alignment between specific preschool learning foundations for social–emotional development and specific health education content standards for kindergarten under *mental, emotional, and social health* may be viewed at (http://www.cde.ca.gov/sp/cd/re/documents/reversealignment.pdf).

The infant/toddler foundations in the social–emotional development domain include key aspects fundamental to the development of self, social interactions, and relationships during the preschool period. Table 2 displays how the infant/toddler foundations *identity of self in relation to others, recognition of ability, expression of emotion, empathy, emotion regulation, impulse control,* and *social understanding* provide the basis for the preschooler's development of the **self.** The infant/toddler foundations *identity of self in relation to others* and *recognition of ability* are the basis for the development of *self-awareness* during the preschool period. Similarly, *emotion regulation, impulse control,* and *attention maintenance* during toddler years undergird children's capacity for *self-regulation* in the preschool years. *Social understanding* at the infant/toddler age continues to develop and corresponds to the preschool substrand *social and emotional understanding,* and the capacity to express *empathy* is linked to the preschool substrand *empathy and caring.* The infant/toddler foundation *recognition of ability,* the ability to make things happen and persist in trying to make things, is aligned with the preschool substrand *initiative in learning.*

The foundations in social–emotional development at the infant/toddler years set the stage for healthy social-emotional competencies during the preschool years. The infant/ toddler foundations also include the competencies involved in **social interaction** with peers and adults and in building positive relationships with others. The infant/toddler foundations *interactions with adults* and *interactions with peers* are aligned with the preschool substrands *interactions with familiar adults* and *interactions with peers.* The preschool foundations also include skills for *group participation* and *cooperation and responsibility,* but these emerge during the preschool years and therefore do not have corresponding infant/toddler foundations. The infant/toddler foundations *relationships with adults* and *relationships with peers* are linked to the preschool substrands under **relationships:** *attachment to parents, friendships,* and *close relationships with teachers and caregivers.*

The kindergarten content standards related to social–emotional development are included as part of the health education standards under the strand **mental, emotional, and social health** rather than as a separate domain. Table 2 shows the correspondence between the strand and substrands in the preschool foundations and the kindergarten standards under *mental, emotional, and social health: essential concepts, analyzing influences, accessing valid information, interpersonal communication, decision making, goal setting, practicing health-enhancing behaviors,* and *health promotion.* For example, the health standard *essential concepts* includes components related to characteristics of self and family, and therefore is aligned with the preschool substrand *self-awareness.* In a similar way, the health standards *goal setting* and *practicing health-enhancing behaviors* focus on showing care, consideration, and concern for others and therefore align with the preschool substrand *empathy and caring.* The content in the preschool substrands *initiative in learning, interaction with familiar adults, group participation, cooperation and responsibility,* and *friendships* is not addressed in the kindergarten content standards: therefore those preschool substrands are not aligned with any kindergarten standards.

Table 2

Overview of the Alignment Between the Social–Emotional Development Domain and the California Content Standards

California Infant/Toddler Learning and Development Foundations	California Preschool Learning Foundations	California Content Standards Kindergarten
Social–Emotional Development	**Social–Emotional Development**	**Health Education**
	Self	**Mental, Emotional, and Social Health**
Identity of Self in Relation to Other Recognition of Ability	Self-Awareness	Essential Concepts
Emotion Regulation Impulse Control Attention Maintenance	Self-Regulation	Interpersonal Communication Practicing Health-Enhancing Behaviors
Social Understanding	Social and Emotional Understanding	Essential Concepts
Empathy	Empathy and Caring	Goal Setting Practicing Health-Enhancing Behaviors
Recognition of Ability	Initiative in Learning	

Table 2 *(continued)*

Social–Emotional Development

California Infant/Toddler Learning and Development Foundations	California Preschool Learning Foundations	California Content Standards Kindergarten
Social–Emotional Development	**Social–Emotional Development**	**Health Education**
	Social Interaction	**Mental, Emotional, and Social Health**
Interactions with Adults →	Interactions with Familiar Adults	
Interactions with Peers →	Interactions with Peers	Interpersonal Communication
	Group Participation	
	Cooperation and Responsibility	
	Relationships	
Relationship with Adults →	Attachment to Parents	
	Close Relationships with Teachers and Caregivers →	Essential Concepts / Analyzing Influences
Relationship with Peers →	Friendships	Accessing Valid Information

Language and Literacy

This section provides an overview of the alignment of the preschool learning foundations in language and literacy with (a) the infant/toddler learning and development foundations; (b) the CCSS in English Language Arts and Literacy in History/Social Studies, Science, and Technical Subjects; and (c) the kindergarten content standards in English–language arts.

(a) Alignment of the Preschool Learning Foundations in Language and Literacy with the Infant/ Toddler Learning and Development Foundations in Language Development

The infant/toddler foundations in the Language Development domain center on four key competencies: *receptive language* (the developing ability to understand language), *expressive language* (the developing ability to produce the sounds of language and use vocabulary and increasingly complex utterances), *communication skills and knowledge* (the developing ability to communicate nonverbally and verbally), and *interest in print* (the developing interest in exploring print in books and the environment). These foundations in language development in the infant/toddler years set the stage for the development of language and literacy skills during the preschool years.

Table 3 presents an overview of the alignment between the preschool learning foundations and the infant/ toddler foundations in language development. As table 3 indicates, the infant/toddler foundation *communication skills and knowledge* continues to develop during the preschool years

and corresponds to the preschool sub-strand *language use and conventions*. *Receptive language* and *expressive language* skills at the infant/toddler age link to preschool children's developing abilities in the substrands of *grammar, vocabulary, phonological awareness,* and *comprehension and analysis of age-appropriate text.* Children's general *interest in print* in the infant/toddler years is the beginning of children's learning and development described by foundations in the preschool sub-strands of *concepts about print, alphabetic and word/print recognition, literacy interest and response,* and *writing strategies.*

(b) Alignment of the Preschool Learning Foundations in Language and Literacy with the CCSS in English Language Arts and Literacy in History/Social Studies, Science, and Technical Subjects

The CCSS specify the progression of skills and understandings, from kindergarten through grade twelve, in two key domains: (a) English Language Arts and Literacy in History/ Social Studies, Science, and Technical Subjects and (b) Mathematics. The following analysis provides an overview of the alignment between the infant/toddler learning and development foundations and the CCSS for kindergarten in the Language and Literacy domain. A detailed alignment between specific preschool learning foundations in Language and Literacy and specific CCSS for kindergarten in language arts and literacy may be viewed at http://www. cde.ca.gov/sp/cd/re/documents/ reversealignment.pdf.

The development of foundational concepts and skills in Language and Literacy during the preschool years relate to children's development of reading, writing, listening, and speaking skills while in kindergarten. The preschool learning foundations in Language and Literacy and the CCSS in English Language Arts are organized according to the same basic categories (strands): **listening and speaking, reading,** and **writing**. The CCSS in English Language Arts and Literacy also include a strand called **language standards**. Each of the strands in the CCSS is organized according to broad, overarching College and Career Readiness (CCR) anchor standards. For each strand, alignment between the preschool learning foundations and the CCSS occurs at both the substrand and the foundation levels. Table 3 shows the alignment between preschool substrands and key areas (CCR anchor standards) in the CCSS for English language arts and literacy.

Table 3 shows that the preschool strand **listening and speaking** is aligned with the CCSS strand **speaking and listening**. The strand **reading** in the preschool foundations is aligned with three sets of **reading** standards in the CCSS: *reading standards for literature, for informational text,* and *in foundational skills* and standards for *speaking and listening.* The preschool strand **writing** is aligned with the CCSS strand **writing**, and the CCSS strand **language standards** is aligned with components in the preschool strand **listening and speaking**.

Table 3 also displays the alignment of the substrands in the preschool foundations with corresponding key areas (CCR anchor standards) in the CCSS. In the strand **listening and**

speaking, the substrand *language use and conventions* is aligned with the CCR anchor standards for speaking and listening: *comprehension and collaboration,* and *presentation of knowledge and ideas.* The preschool substrands *vocabulary* and *grammar* are aligned with the CCR anchor standards for language: *vocabulary acquisition and use,* and *conventions of standard English,* respectively. The **reading** substrands in the preschool foundations are aligned with the CCR anchor standards for reading: *key ideas and details, craft and structure,* and *integration of knowledge and ideas,* and with the CCSS reading standards: foundational skills in the areas of *phonological awareness, print concepts, phonics and word recognition.*

The CCSS reading standards for kindergarten—*fluency* and *range of reading and level of text complexity*—present skills that emerge in kindergarten and therefore have no corresponding foundations at the preschool level. Table 3 shows the specific alignment of the reading substrands with the CCR anchor standards for reading. Finally, the substrand *writing strategies* is aligned with the CCR anchor standard *text types and purposes.* Additional CCSS writing standards for kindergarten exist in the areas of *production and distribution of writing* and *research to build and represent knowledge,* but these do not have corresponding foundations at the preschool level. All preschool substrands are aligned with corresponding CCSS, except for the substrand *literacy interest and response.*

Table 3

Overview of the Alignment Between the Language and Literacy Domain and the Common Core State Standards

Language and Literacy

California Infant/Toddler Learning and Development Foundations	California Preschool Learning Foundations	Common Core State Standards Kindergarten
Language Development	**Language and Literacy**	**English Language Arts & Literacy in History/Social Studies, Science, and Technical Subjects**
	Listening and Speaking	Speaking and Listening Standards
Communication Skills and Knowledge	Language Use and Conventions	Comprehension and Collaboration
		Presentation of Knowledge and Ideas
		Language Standards
Receptive Language	Vocabulary	Vocabulary Acquisition and Use
Expressive Language	Grammar	Conventions of Standard English
	Reading	Reading Standards for Literature
		Reading Standards for Informational Text
		Reading Standards: Foundational Skills
		Speaking and Listening Standards
Receptive Language	Phonological Awareness	Phonological Awareness
Expressive Language	Comprehension and Analysis of Age-Appropriate Text	Key Ideas and Details
		Integration of Knowledge and Ideas
		Comprehension and Collaboration

Table 3 *(continued)*

Language and Literacy

California Infant/Toddler Learning and Development Foundations	California Preschool Learning Foundations	Common Core State Standards Kindergarten
Language Development	**Language and Literacy**	**English Language Arts & Literacy in History/Social Studies, Science, and Technical Subjects**
	Reading	**Reading Standards for Literature** **Reading Standards for Informational Text** **Reading Standards: Foundational Skills** **Speaking and Listening Standards**
Interest in Print ⬆	Concepts about Print ⬆	Print Concepts Craft and Structure
	Alphabetics and Word/ Print Recognition	Print Concepts Phonics and Word Recognition
	Literacy Interest and Response	
	Writing	**Writing Standards**
Interest in Print ⬆	Writing Strategies ⬆	Text Types and Purposes

(c) Alignment of the Preschool Learning Foundations in Language and Literacy with the Kindergarten Content Standards in English–Language Arts

Table 4 provides an overview of the alignment between the preschool learning foundations in Language and Literacy and the kindergarten content standards in English–language arts. A detailed alignment between specific preschool learning foundations for Language and Literacy and specific kindergarten content standards for English–language arts may be viewed at http://www.cde.ca.gov/sp/cd/re/documents/reversealignment.pdf.

The development of foundational concepts and skills in language and literacy during the preschool years relate to children's development of reading, writing, listening, and speaking skills while in kindergarten. The preschool learning foundations in language and literacy and the kindergarten content standards in English–language arts are organized according to the same basic categories (strands): **listening and speaking**, **reading,** and **writing**. The kindergarten content standards also include a strand called **written and oral English language conventions.** For each strand, alignment between the preschool learning foundations and the kindergarten content standards occurs at both the substrand and foundation/content standard levels.

Table 4 shows how the preschool learning foundations substrand of

language use and conventions corresponds to the kindergarten content standards of *listening and speaking strategies, speaking applications, and written and oral English language conventions.* The eight remaining substrands of the preschool learning foundations link to the substrands of the kindergarten content standards in the following way: *grammar* aligns with *written and oral English language conventions (sentence structure); vocabulary* aligns with *vocabulary and concept development; phonological awareness* aligns with *phonemic awareness; comprehension and analysis of age-appropriate text* aligns with *comprehension and analysis of grade-level-appropriate text* and with *narrative analysis of grade-level-appropriate text.* Concepts *about print* align with *concepts about print, structural features of informational materials,* and *narrative analysis of grade-level-appropriate text; alphabetic and word/print recognition* aligns with *concepts about print* and *decoding and word recognition;* and *writing strategies* align with *writing strategies.* In summary, for almost every substrand of preschool learning foundations, there is at least one substrand of kindergarten content standards that reflects the content of those preschool foundations. *Literacy interest and response* is the only preschool foundation substrand that does not align with any of the kindergarten content standards.

Table 4

Overview of the Alignment Between the Language and Literacy Domain and the California Content Standards

Language and Literacy

California Infant/Toddler Learning and Development Foundations	California Preschool Learning Foundations	California Content Standards Kindergarten
Language Development	**Language and Literacy**	**English–Language Arts**

Language Development

Communication Skills and Knowledge

Receptive Language
Expressive Language → Grammar

Language and Literacy

Listening and Speaking

Language Use and Conventions

Vocabulary

English–Language Arts

Listening and Speaking

Listening and Speaking Strategies: *Comprehension*

Speaking Applications

Written and Oral English Language Conventions

Written and Oral Language Conventions: *Sentence Structure*

Written and Oral English Language Conventions

Written and Oral Language Conventions: *Sentence Structure*

Reading

Word Analysis, Fluency, and Systematic Vocabulary Development: *Vocabulary and Concept Development*

Listening and Speaking

Speaking Applications

Table 4 (continued)

Language and Literacy

California Infant/Toddler Learning and Development Foundations	California Preschool Learning Foundations	California Content Standards Kindergarten
Language Development	**Language and Literacy**	**English–Language Arts**
	Reading	Reading
Receptive Language, Expressive Language →	Phonological Awareness	→ Word Analysis, Fluency, and Systematic Vocabulary Development: *Phonemic Awareness*
		→ Reading Comprehension: *Comprehension and Analysis of Grade-Level-Appropriate Text*
	Comprehension and Analysis of Age-Appropriate Text	→ Literacy Response and Analysis: *Narrative Analysis of Grade-Level-Appropriate Text*
		→ Word Analysis, Fluency, and Systematic Vocabulary Development: *Concepts About Print*
	Concepts about Print	→ Reading Comprehension: *Structural Features of Informational Materials*
		→ Literacy Response and Analysis: *Narrative Analysis of Grade-Level-Appropriate Text*
Interest in Print →	Alphabetics and Word/Print Recognition	→ Word Analysis, Fluency, and Systematic Vocabulary Development: *Concepts About Print; Decoding and Word Recognition*
	Literacy Interest and Response	

Table 4 *(continued)*

Language and Literacy

California Infant/Toddler Learning and Development Foundations	California Preschool Learning Foundations	California Content Standards Kindergarten
Language Development	**Language and Literacy**	**English–Language Arts**
	Writing	**Writing**
	Writing Strategies	Writing Strategies: Organization and Focus; *Penmanship*
Interest in Print →	→	**Written and Oral English Language Conventions**
		Written and Oral English Language Conventions: *Spelling*

English-Language Development

This section provides an overview of the alignment of the preschool foundations in English-Language Development (ELD) with the infant/toddler foundations in Language Development and with the kindergarten content standards for California public schools in ELD.

Children's language and literacy skills in their first language contribute to acquiring English. Children who are English-language learners transfer the skills of their home language to the process of learning English. The alignment draws the connection between the infant/toddler foundations in Language Development and the preschool foundations in ELD. As table 5 indicates, the development of children's receptive and expressive language skills, communication skills, and interest in print in their home language provides the foundation for their development of listening, speaking, reading, and writing skills in English. The infant/toddler foundation *receptive language* is aligned with the preschool ELD strand **listening;** the infant/toddler foundation *expressive language* is aligned with the preschool ELD strand **speaking.** The foundation *communication skills and knowledge* corresponds to the preschool substrand of *understanding and using social conventions in English,* and the infant/toddler foundation *interest in print* is aligned with the ELD strands **reading** and **writing.**

Table 5 also presents the alignment of the preschool foundations in ELD with the K–12 standards for ELD. The four strands (listening, speaking, reading and writing) in the preschool foundations for ELD are aligned with the content categories of California's ELD standards (listening and speaking, reading, writing) in K–12. The K–12 ELD standards have three levels: beginning, intermediate, and advanced. Similarly, the preschool foundations in ELD are defined at the beginning, middle, and later stages of English acquisition.

The K–12 ELD standards do not necessarily represent a developmental progression from preschool to kindergarten. The K–12 ELD standards apply to different aspects of children's individual levels of English acquisition. Consequently, it is not appropriate to align specific preschool foundations with specific kindergarten standards in the ELD domain. The alignment points only to corresponding content areas (substrands) in the preschool foundations and the K–12 ELD standards; it does not identify the next level of English acquisition for children entering kindergarten. Therefore, there is no table aligning specific preschool foundations with specific K–12 standards in the ELD domain.

The alignment draws upon the parallel content areas between the preschool foundations in ELD and the K–12 standards in ELD. As table 5 shows, for almost every substrand of preschool learning foundations in ELD, there is at least one substrand of the kindergarten content standards that reflects the content of those preschool foundations. Two substrands in the preschool learning foundations have no corresponding content in the K–12 standards in ELD: *Children demonstrate an appreciation and enjoyment of reading and literature* and *Children demonstrate awareness that print carries meaning.*

Table 5

Overview of the Alignment Between the English-Language Development Domain and the California Content Standards

English Language Development		
California Infant/Toddler Learning and Development Foundations	**California Preschool Learning Foundations**	**California Content Standards Kindergarten**
Language Development	**English-Language Development**	**K–12 English-Language Development Standards**

Language Development

Receptive Language → **Listening** → Children listen with understanding. →

Listening and Speaking

Strategies and Applications: Comprehension

Reading

Word Analysis, Fluency, and Systematic Vocabulary Development: *Vocabulary and Concept Development*

Expressive Language → **Speaking** →
- Children use nonverbal and verbal strategies to communicate with others.
- Children use language to create oral narratives about their personal experiences.

→ **Listening and Speaking**

Strategies and Applications: *Organization and Delivery of Oral Communication*

Reading

Word Analysis, Fluency, and Systematic Vocabulary Development: *Vocabulary and Concept Development*

Communication Skills and Knowledge → Children begin to understand and use social conventions in English. → **Listening and Speaking**

Strategies and Applications: *Organization and Delivery of Oral Communication*

Table 5 *(continued)*

English Language Development

California Infant/Toddler Learning and Development Foundations	California Preschool Learning Foundations	California Content Standards Kindergarten	K–12 English-Language Development Standards
Language Development	**English-Language Development**		**English-Language Development Standards**

Reading

California Infant/Toddler Learning and Development Foundations	California Preschool Learning Foundations	K–12 English-Language Development Standards
Interest in Print →	Children demonstrate an appreciation and enjoyment of reading and literature. / Children show an increasing understanding of book reading. →	Reading Comprehension: *Comprehension and Analysis of Grade-Level-Appropriate Text; Structural Features of Informational Materials*
	Children demonstrate an understanding of print conventions. →	Reading Comprehension: *Comprehension and Analysis of Grade-Level-Appropriate Text*
	Children demonstrate awareness that print carries meaning.	
	Children demonstrate progress in their knowledge of the alphabet in English. / Children demonstrate phonological awareness. →	Word Analysis, Fluency, and Systematic Vocabulary Development: *Phonemic Awareness; Decoding and Word Recognition*
Expressive Language →		

Writing

California Infant/Toddler Learning and Development Foundations	California Preschool Learning Foundations	K–12 English-Language Development Standards
Interest in Print →	Children use writing to communicate their ideas. →	Strategies and Applications: *Penmanship; Organization and Focus*

Mathematics

This section provides an overview of the alignment of the preschool learning foundations in Mathematics with (a) the infant/toddler learning and development foundations in Cognitive Development, (b) the CCSS for mathematics, and (c) the kindergarten content standards for mathematics.

(a) Alignment of the Preschool Learning Foundations in Mathematics with the Infant/ Toddler Learning and Development Foundations in Cognitive Development

A range of core mathematical abilities identified in the preschool learning foundations in Mathematics emerge and begin to develop during the infant/toddler years. Five of the infant/toddler foundations in Cognitive Development center on key mathematical concepts and skills: *number sense, classification, understanding of personal care routines, spatial relationships,* and *problem solving.* These foundations in Cognitive Development during the infant/toddler years set the stage for the development of mathematical skills during the preschool years.

Table 6 shows how the infant/toddler foundation *number sense* corresponds to the preschool substrands related to *number sense,* focusing on children's understanding of quantity, number relationships, and operations (addition and subtraction). Similarly, the infant/toddler foundation *classification* corresponds to the preschool substrand *classification,* focusing on children's continuous development of the ability to sort and classify objects in their everyday environment. The infant/toddler foundation *understand-*

ing of personal care routine is linked to children's ability to identify simple repeating patterns. The daily routine follows a pattern, and children are able to anticipate and or predict what comes next. *Spatial relationships,* the developing understanding in the infant/toddler years of how things move and fit in space, set the stage for children's learning about *shapes* and *positions in space* (geometry strand) and about *comparing, ordering* and *measuring objects* (measurement strand). The development of *problem-solving* skills in the infant/toddler years is linked to children's *mathematical reasoning,* the ability to use mathematical thinking to solve problems that arise in their everyday environment.

(b) Alignment of the Preschool Learning Foundations in Mathematics with the Common Core State Standards in Mathematics

The foundations and the CCSS in Mathematics cover the same key areas of learning. The first four strands in the preschool foundations in Mathematics are aligned with CCSS for *mathematical content.* The preschool strand **number sense** is aligned with the CCSS categories: *counting and cardinality, operations and algebraic thinking,* and *number and operations in base ten.*

The preschool strand **algebra and functions (classification and patterning)** is aligned with components in the CCSS category of *measurement and data.* Content related to classification appears under **algebra and functions** in the preschool foundations and under **measurement and data** in the CCSS. The preschool strand **measurement** is aligned with the CCSS of *measurement and data,* and the strand

geometry is directly aligned with the CCSS cluster of standards in *geometry*. The last preschool strand, **mathematical reasoning,** is aligned with the CCSS for *mathematical practices*. Table 6 shows the alignment between strands and substrands in the preschool foundations and the content categories in the CCSS for Mathematics. The detailed alignment between specific preschool foundations and specific kindergarten standards in the CCSS for Mathematics may be viewed at http://www.cde.ca.gov/sp/cd/re/documents/reversealignment.pdf.

For every substrand of the preschool learning foundations, there is a category in the CCSS with corresponding content. The substrands under **number sense**—*understanding numbers and quantities* and *understanding number relationships and operations*—correspond directly to the CCSS in the categories *counting and cardinality* and *operations and algebraic thinking,* respectively. Content in *number and operations in base ten* of the CCSS is too advanced for there to be corresponding content in the preschool foundations. The preschool substrand addressing *sorting and classifying objects* aligns with the CCSS of *classify objects and count the number of objects in each category*. However, preschool substrand 2.0 on patterning has no corresponding content in the CCSS. The preschool strand on **measurement,** about comparing, ordering, and measuring objects, is aligned with the kindergarten CCSS of *Describe and compare measurable attributes*. The preschool substrand under **geometry** *(Children identify and use a variety of shapes in their environment)* is aligned with the standards in the CCSS categories under geometry: *Identify and describe shapes* and *Analyze, compare, create, and compose shapes*. Finally, the preschool substrand *Children use mathematical thinking to solve problems,* under the strand **mathematical reasoning** is aligned with the CCSS for mathematical practices. These include processes that involve mathematical problem solving such as *Make sense of problems and persevere in solving them,* and *Reason abstractly and quantitatively.*

Table 6

Overview of the Alignment Between the Mathematics Domain and the Common Core State Standards

California Infant/Toddler Learning and Development Foundations	California Preschool Learning Foundations	Common Core State Standards Kindergarten
Cognitive Development	**Mathematics**	**Mathematics**

Mathematics

	Number Sense	**Counting and Cardinality**
	Children understand numbers and quantities in their everyday environment. →	Know number names and the count sequence
		Count to tell the number of objects
Number Sense →		Compare numbers
	Children understand number relationships and operations in their everyday environment. →	**Operations and Algebraic Thinking**
		Understand addition as putting together and adding to, and subtraction as taking apart and taking from
		Number and Operations in Base Ten
		Work with numbers 11–19 to gain foundations for place value

	Algebra and Functions (Classification and Patterning)	**Measurement and Data**
Classification →	Children sort and classify objects in their everyday environment. →	Classify objects and count the number of objects in categories
Understanding of Personal Routine →	Children recognize/expand understanding of simple repeating patterns. →	

Table 6 *(continued)*

Mathematics

California Infant/Toddler Learning and Development Foundations	California Preschool Learning Foundations	Common Core State Standards Kindergarten
Cognitive Development	**Mathematics**	**Mathematics**
	Measurement	**Measurement and Data**
Spatial Relationships →	Children compare, order, and measure objects. →	Describe and compare measurable attributes
	Geometry	**Geometry**
Spatial Relationships →	Children identify and use shapes. →	Identify and describe shapes (squares, circles, triangles, rectangles, hexagons, cubes, cones, cylinders, and spheres).
		Analyze, compare, create, and compose shapes.
	Children understand positions in space. →	Identify and describe shapes (squares, circles, triangles, rectangles, hexagons, cubes, cones, cylinders, and spheres).

Table 6 *(continued)*

Mathematics

California Infant/Toddler Learning and Development Foundations	California Preschool Learning Foundations	Common Core State Standards Kindergarten
Cognitive Development	**Mathematics**	**Mathematics**
Problem Solving	Mathematical Reasoning	**Standards for Mathematical Practice (K-12)**
	Children use mathematical thinking to solve problems in their everyday environment.	Make sense of problems and persevere in solving them.
		Reason abstractly and quantitatively.
		Construct viable arguments and critique the reasoning of others.
		Model with mathematics.
		Use appropriate tools strategically.
		Attend to precision.
		Look for and make use of structure.
		Look for and express regularity in repeated reasoning.

(c) Alignment of the Preschool Learning Foundations in Mathematics with the Mathematics Content Standards for Kindergarten

The foundations and the kindergarten standards cover the same general categories (strands): **number sense**, **algebra and functions (classification and patterning)**, **measurement**, **geometry**, and **mathematical reasoning**. In the kindergarten content standards, there is an additional strand: **statistics, data analysis, and probability**, which focuses on data collection and patterning. In addition, kindergarten standards in measurement and geometry are combined into one strand, **measurement and geometry,** rather than divided into two separate strands. Table 7 shows the alignment between strands and substrands in the preschool foundations and the kindergarten strands and substrands. The detailed alignment between specific preschool foundations and specific kindergarten content standards for Mathematics may be viewed at http://www.cde.ca.gov/sp/cd/re/documents/reversealignment.pdf.

As table 7 indicates, the strands in the preschool foundations correspond directly to strands in the kindergarten standards. For every substrand of the preschool learning foundations, there are kindergarten content standards that reflect the content of those preschool foundations. The substrands under **number sense,** *understanding numbers and quantities* and *understanding number relationships and operations*, correspond directly to the kindergarten content standards of **number sense:** *Students understand the relationships between numbers and quantities,* and *students understand and describe simple additions and subtractions.* The substrand addressing *sorting and classifying objects* aligns with the kindergarten substrand *Students sort and classify objects, and the patterning substrand* aligns with the kindergarten substrand *Students collect information about objects and events in their environment.* The preschool strand on **measurement** (about comparing, ordering, and measuring objects) is aligned with the kindergarten substrand under measurement and geometry in which *students understand that objects have properties, such as length, weight, and capacity, and that comparisons may be made by referring to those properties.* The preschool substrand under **geometry,** *Children identify and use a variety of shapes in their environment,* is aligned with the second kindergarten substrand under measurement and geometry: *Students identify common objects in their environment and describe the geometric features.* The preschool geometry substrand on the understanding of positions in space is aligned with substrands outside the mathematics domain. It is directly related to kindergarten content in the physical education standards for *movement concepts,* and in history–social science: *Students compare and contrast the locations of people, places, and environments and describe their characteristics.* Finally, the preschool strand *mathematical reasoning* matches the kindergarten strand *mathematical reasoning.*

Table 7

Overview of the Alignment Between the Mathematics Domain and the California Content Standards

California Infant/Toddler Learning and Development Foundations	California Preschool Learning Foundations	California Content Standards Kindergarten
Cognitive Development	**Mathematics**	**Mathematics**
Number Sense →	**Number Sense**	**Number Sense**
	Children understand numbers and quantities in their everyday environment. →	Students understand the relationship between numbers and quantities.
	Children understand number relationships and operations in their everyday environment. →	Students understand the relationship between numbers and quantities.
		Students understand and describe simple additions and subtractions.
Classification →	**Algebra and Functions**	**Algebra and Functions**
	Children sort and classify objects in their everyday environment. →	Students sort and classify objects.
Understanding of Personal Routine →	Children recognize/expand understanding of simple repeating patterns. →	**Statistics, Data Analysis, and Probability**
		Students collect information about objects and events in their environment.

Table 7 *(continued)*

Mathematics

California Infant/Toddler Learning and Development Foundations	California Preschool Learning Foundations	California Content Standards Kindergarten
Cognitive Development	**Mathematics**	**Mathematics**
	Measurement	**Measurement and Geometry**
Spatial Relationships →	Children compare, order, and measure objects. →	Students understand that objects have properties, such as length, weight, and capacity, and that comparisons may be made by referring to those properties.
	Geometry	**Measurement and Geometry**
	Children identify and use shapes. →	Students identify common objects in their environment and describe the geometric features.
Spatial Relationships →	Children understand positions in space. →	**Domain: Physical Education** **Standard 2** *Movement Concepts* Students demonstrate knowledge of movement concepts, principles, and strategies that apply to the learning and performance of physical activities. **Domain: History–Social Science** K.4 Students compare and contrast the locations of people, places, and environments and describe their characteristics.

Table 7 (continued)

Mathematics

California Infant/Toddler Learning and Development Foundations	California Preschool Learning Foundations	California Content Standards Kindergarten
Cognitive Development	**Mathematics**	**Mathematics**
	Mathematical Reasoning	**Mathematical Reasoning**
Problem Solving →	Children use mathematical thinking to solve problems in their everyday environment. →	Students make decisions about how to set up a problem.
		Students solve problems in reasonable ways and justify their reasoning.

Visual and Performing Arts

This section describes the alignment of the preschool foundations in the Visual and Performing Arts with the infant/toddler learning and development foundations and the California content standards for kindergarten in the Visual and Performing Arts (visual arts, music, theatre, and dance).

The skills and knowledge in the Visual and Performing Arts are built on ones that children develop in the Language, Perceptual, Motor, Cognitive, and Social–Emotional Development domains. Whether children improvise vocally and instrumentally or act out with others through music and movement, the visual arts, music, drama, and dance tap children's intellectual, social, and physical competencies. Children's developing capacity to communicate, express themselves verbally, move their bodies with competence, engage in symbolic play, interact with peers and adults cooperatively, along with other skills, form the foundation of their development in the Visual and Performing Arts. For this reason, as table 8 indicates, the Visual and Performing Arts domain is aligned with all four developmental domains in the infant/toddler foundations: Social–Emotional Development, Language Development, Cognitive Development, and Perceptual and Motor Development. Each domain plays a role in children's development in the Visual and Performing Arts.

The preschool learning foundations in visual art, music, drama, and dance are also aligned with the kindergarten content standards in the corresponding domains: **Visual Arts, Music, Theatre,** and **Dance**. The kindergarten content standards in each artistic domain are organized by the following main categories (strands): **artistic perception, creative expression, historical and cultural context, aesthetic valuing,** and **connections, relationships, applications**. Table 8 shows the alignment between preschool substrands and kindergarten strands in Visual Arts, Music, Theatre, and Dance. The detailed alignment between specific preschool foundations and specific kindergarten content standards in the Visual and Performing Arts domains may be viewed at http://www.cde.ca.gov/sp/cd/re/documents/reversealignment.pdf.

In general, the preschool substrand *notice, respond, and engage,* in each artistic discipline, is aligned with the kindergarten strands *artistic perception* and *aesthetic valuing.* In some strands, the preschool substrand *notice, respond, and engage* is also aligned with components of the kindergarten strand *historical and cultural context.* The other two preschool substrands— *develop skills* and *create, invent, and express*—are aligned with the kindergarten strand **creative expression.** As table 8 indicates, for every substrand of the preschool learning foundations in the Visual and Performing Arts, there is at least one substrand of the kindergarten content standards that reflects the content of the corresponding preschool foundations.

Table 8

Overview of the Alignment Between the Visual and Performing Arts Domain and the California Content Standards

California Infant/Toddler Learning and Development Foundations	California Preschool Learning Foundations	California Content Standards Kindergarten
Visual and Performing Arts	**Visual and Performing Arts**	**Visual and Performing Arts: Visual Arts, Music, Theatre, and Dance**
	Visual Art	**Visual Art**
Social–Emotional Development Language Development Cognitive Development Perceptual and Motor Development →	Notice, Respond, and Engage →	Artistic Perception: *Develop Perceptual Skills and Visual Arts Vocabulary; Analyze Art Elements and Principles of Design* Historical and Cultural Context: *Diversity of the Visual Arts* Aesthetic Valuing: *Derive Meaning; Make Informed Judgments*
	Develop Skills in Visual Art →	Creative Expression: *Skills, Processes, Materials, and Tools; Communication and Expression Through Original Works of Art* Artistic Perception: *Develop Perceptual Skills and Visual Arts Vocabulary*
	Create, Invent, and Express Through Visual Art →	Creative Expression: *Communication and Expression Through Original Works of Art*

Table 8 *(continued)*

Visual and Performing Arts

California Infant/Toddler Learning and Development Foundations	California Preschool Learning Foundations	California Content Standards Kindergarten
Visual and Performing Arts	Visual and Performing Arts	Visual and Performing Arts: Visual Arts, Music, Theatre, and Dance
Music	**Music**	**Music**
Social–Emotional Development	Notice, Respond, and Engage	Artistic Perception: *Listen to, Analyze, and Describe Music*
Language Development	Develop Skills in Music	Historical and Cultural Context: *Diversity of Music*
Cognitive Development	Create, Invent, and Express Through Music	Aesthetic Valuing: *Derive Meaning*
Perceptual and Motor Development		Creative Expression: *Apply Vocal and Instrumental Skills*
		Creative Expression: *Compose, Arrange, and Improvise*
		Aesthetic Valuing: *Derive Meaning*
	Drama	**Theatre**
Social–Emotional Development	Notice, Respond, and Engage	Artistic Perception: *Development of the Vocabulary of Theatre; Comprehension and Analysis of the Elements of Theatre*
Language Development	Develop Skill Used to Create, Invent, and Express Through Drama	Aesthetic Valuing: *Critical Assessment of Theatre; Derivation of Meaning from Works of Theatre*
Cognitive Development		Creative Expression: *Development of Theatrical Skills; Creation/Invention in Theatre*
Perceptual and Motor Development		Historical and Cultural Context: *Role and Cultural Significance of Theatre*

Table 8 *(continued)*

Visual and Performing Arts

California Infant/Toddler Learning and Development Foundations	California Preschool Learning Foundations	California Content Standards Kindergarten
	Visual and Performing Arts	**Visual and Performing Arts: Visual Arts, Music, Theatre, and Dance**
	Dance	**Dance**
Social–Emotional Development Language Development Cognitive Development Perceptual and Motor Development →	Notice, Respond, and Engage →	*Artistic Perception: Development of Motor Skills and Technical Expertise; Comprehension and Analysis of Dance Elements; Development of Dance Vocabulary* *Aesthetic Valuing: Description, Analysis, and Criticism of Dance*
	Develop Skills in Dance →	*Artistic Perception: Development of Motor Skill and Technical Expertise* **Domain: Physical Education** **Standard 1** *Movement Concepts; Rhythmic Skills* **Standard 2** Movement Concepts
	Create, Invent, and Express Through Dance →	*Creative Expression: Creation/Invention of Dance Movements*

Physical Development

This section describes an overview of the alignment of the preschool foundations in Physical Development with the infant/toddler learning and development foundations in the domains of Perceptual–Motor Development and Cognitive Development, and with the physical education content standards in kindergarten. Table 9 shows how the strands and substrands of the preschool learning foundations in Physical Development align with infant/toddler foundations in the Perceptual and Motor and the Cognitive Development domains and with the physical education content standards for kindergarten. The detailed alignment between specific preschool learning foundations in Physical Development and specific kindergarten content standards in physical education may be viewed at http://www.cde.ca.gov/sp/cd/re/docuemnts/reversealignment.pdf.

Core concepts and a range of skills identified in the preschool learning foundations in Physical Development emerge and develop during the infant/toddler years. The infant/toddler foundations in Perceptual and Motor Development (gross motor, fine motor, and perceptual development) and the Cognitive Development foundation (spatial relationships) set the stage for the development of key skills and concepts in Physical Development during the preschool years. Table 9 displays the alignment between the infant/toddler foundations in Perceptual and Motor Development and spatial relationships, and the strands and substrands covered in the preschool learning foundations in Physical Development. As table 9 indicates, the infant/toddler foundation gross motor is aligned with the substrands balance and locomotor skills, and the foundation fine motor corresponds to the preschool substrand manipulative skills. Perceptual development and spatial relationships set the stage for children's development of spatial awareness and directional awareness.

The preschool learning foundations in Physical Development are also aligned with the physical education content standards in kindergarten. The kindergarten standards consist of five main standards in the following areas:

- K.1 — motor skills and movement patterns
- K.2 — knowledge of movement concepts, principles, and strategies
- K.3 — level of physical fitness
- K.4 — knowledge of physical fitness concepts, principles, and strategies
- K.5 — knowledge of psychological and sociological concepts, principles, and strategies that apply to the learning and performance of physical activity

The standards cover a broad range of concepts and skills organized by categories such as movement concepts, body management, locomotor movement, manipulative skills, rhythmic skills, fitness concepts, and aerobic capacity. The kindergarten standards K.1–K.4 in physical education are aligned with the preschool foundations in Physical Development. Kindergarten standard K.5 involves knowledge and skills that are not reflected in the preschool foundations in Physical Development and therefore is not included in this alignment. Table 9 shows the alignment between strands and substrands in the domain of Physical Development with key content standards for kindergarten in physical education. For every strand and substrand in the preschool learning foundations in Physical Development, there are kindergarten content standards that reflect the content of those preschool foundations. The strands **fundamental movement skills** and **perceptual–motor skills and movement concepts** are aligned with the kindergarten physical education standards focusing on skills and knowledge of movement (standards K.1 and K.2). The strand **active physical play** is aligned with the kindergarten standards focusing on skills and knowledge of physical fitness (standards K.3 and K.4).

Table 9 also displays the correspondence between the preschool substrands and the categories of concepts and skills covered in each of the kindergarten standards in physical education. The substrand *balance* corresponds to skills in the category of *body management;* the substrand *loco-motor skills* is aligned with kindergarten category *locomotor movement;* and the substrand *manipulative skills* corresponds directly to the kindergarten category *manipulative skills.* Similarly, in the second strand of the preschool foundations, the substrand *body awareness* is aligned with *body management;* the substrand *spatial awareness* is aligned with the kindergarten category *movement concepts;* and the concepts and skills in the substrand *directional awareness* correspond to skills and concepts in two categories of kindergarten standards: *body management* and *movement concepts.* Finally, in the strand of active physical play, the substrand *active participation* is aligned with *fitness concepts; cardiovascular endurance* is aligned with *aerobic capacity;* and the substrand *muscular strength, muscular endurance, and flexibility* is directly aligned with the kindergarten categories *muscular strength/endurance* and *flexibility.*

Table 9

Overview of the Alignment Between the Physical Development Domain and the California Content Standards

California Infant/Toddler Learning and Development Foundations	California Preschool Learning Foundations	California Content Standards Kindergarten
Physical Development	**Physical Development**	**Physical Education**
Perceptual and Motor Development Also aligned with elements from: **Cognitive Development**	**Fundamental Movement Skills**	**Standard 1:** Motor Skills and Movement Patterns **Standard 2:** Knowledge of Movement Concepts
Gross Motor →	Balance →	Body Management (Standard 1)
Fine Motor →	Locomotor Skills →	Locomotor Movement (Standards 1 and 2)
	Manipulative Skills →	Manipulative Skills (Standard 1)
	Perceptual Motor Skills and Movement Concepts	**Standard 1:** Motor Skills and Movement Patterns **Standard 2:** Knowledge of Movement Concepts
Spatial Relationships (Cognitive Development) →	Body Awareness →	Body Management (Standard 2)
Perceptual Development (Cognitive Development) →	Spatial Awareness →	Movement Concepts (Standards 1 and 2)
	Directional Awareness →	Body Management (Standard 1)
		Movement Concepts (Standards 1 and 2)

Table 9 *(continued)*

Physical Development

California Infant/Toddler Learning and Development Foundations	California Preschool Learning Foundations	California Content Standards Kindergarten
Perceptual and Motor Development Also aligned with elements from: **Cognitive Development**	**Physical Development**	**Physical Education**
	Active Physical Play	**Standard 3:** Level of Physical Fitness **Standard 4:** Knowledge of Physical Fitness Concepts
	Active Participation →	Fitness Concepts (Standards 3 and 4)
	Cardiovascular Endurance →	Aerobic Capacity (Standards 3 and 4)
	Muscular Strength, Muscular Endurance, and Flexibility →	Muscular Strength/Endurance (Standards 3 and 4) Flexibility (Standards 3 and 4)

Health

This section describes an overview of the alignment of the preschool foundations in health science with the infant/toddler learning and development foundations and the California health education content standards for kindergarten. The detailed alignment between specific preschool learning foundations in Health and specific kindergarten content standards in Health Education may be viewed at http://www.cde.ca.gov/sp/cd/re/documents/reversealignment.pdf.

The basic skills and concepts acquired during the infant/toddler years set the stage for the development of health behaviors and concepts during the preschool years. Whether washing hands, communicating to an adult about not feeling well, following emergency routines, or demonstrating knowledge of body parts, children practice health habits and understand concepts that draw on cognitive, language, social, and physical competencies. Children's developing capacity to communicate, establish relationships with adults in the environment, understand and participate in personal care routines, reason about cause and effect, perform fine-motor manipulative activities, and acquire other skills forms the foundation of health concepts, skills, and behaviors. For this reason, as shown in Table 10, the preschool health domain is aligned with all four developmental domains in the infant/toddler foundations: Social–Emotional Development, Language Development, Cognitive Development, and Perceptual and Motor Development. Each domain plays a role in children's development of health practices, knowledge, and skills.

As children grow, they develop a deeper understanding of the concepts related to health and illness; have a greater ability to practice health-enhancing behaviors; and communicate and reason about health concepts. The kindergarten standards in health education cover a broader range of content areas, and include more aspects of health concepts, behaviors, and skills. The health education standards in kindergarten are organized according to the following categories (strands): **nutrition and physical activity; growth and development; injury prevention and safety, alcohol, tobacco, and other drugs; mental, emotional and social health;** and **personal and community health.** Table 10 shows the alignment of the kindergarten strands in health education with the strands in the preschool foundations. The first preschool strand, **health habits,** is aligned with two of the kindergarten strands (**personal and community health** and **growth and development**). The preschool strand, **safety,** is aligned with the kindergarten strand **injury prevention and safety,** and **nutrition** is aligned with the kindergarten strand **nutrition and physical activity.** The content in the kindergarten strand **alcohol, tobacco, and other drugs** is not addressed in the preschool foundations; therefore that strand is not part of the alignment. The content in the kindergarten strand **mental, emotional, and social health** maps to the content in the preschool foundations in Social–Emotional Development; therefore, it is aligned with the preschool foundations in Social–Emotional Development rather than with the Health foundations.

Each strand in the kindergarten standards in health education includes standards related to key areas in health: *essential concepts, analyzing influences, accessing valid information, interpersonal communication, decision making, goal setting, practicing health-enhancing behaviors, and health promotion.* Table 10 also displays the alignment between the substrands in the preschool foundations in Health and the kindergarten standards in health education. For example, the preschool substrands *basic hygiene* and *oral health* are aligned with two kindergarten standards in personal and community health: *essential concepts* and *practicing health-enhancing behaviors.* As Table 10 indicates, for every strand and substrand in the preschool learning foundations in health there is a corresponding category of kindergarten content standards, with the exception of the preschool substrand *self-regulation of eating.*

Table 10

Overview of the Alignment Between the Health Domain and the California Content Standards

California Infant/Toddler Learning and Development Foundations	California Preschool Learning Foundations	California Content Standards Kindergarten
Health		
	Health	**Health Education**

Health Habits → **Personal and Community Health Growth and Development**

Basic Hygiene
→ **Personal and Community Health**
　Essential Concepts
　Practicing Health-Enhancing Behaviors

Oral Health
→ **Personal and Community Health**
　Essential Concepts
　Practicing Health-Enhancing Behavior

Knowledge of Wellness
→ **Growth and Development**
　Essential Concepts
→ **Personal and Community Health**
　Accessing Valid Information
　Interpersonal Communication

Sun Safety
→ **Personal and Community Health**
　Essential Concepts

Social–Emotional Development
Language Development
Cognitive Development
Perceptual and Motor Development
→

Table 10 *(continued)*

Health

California Infant/Toddler Learning and Development Foundations	California Preschool Learning Foundations	California Content Standards Kindergarten

Health Education

Health	Safety	Injury Prevention and Safety

Injury Prevention and Safety

- Essential Concepts
- Accessing Valid Information
- Interpersonal Communication
- Decision Making
- Practicing Health-Enhancing Behaviors

Safety

Injury Prevention

- Social–Emotional Development
- Language Development
- Cognitive Development
- Perceptual and Motor Development

Nutrition and Physical Activity

- Essential Concepts
- Essential Concepts
- Analyzing Influences
- Interpersonal Communication
- Practicing Health-Enhancing Behaviors

Nutrition

- Nutrition Knowledge
- Nutrition Choices
- Self-Regulation of Eating

- Social–Emotional Development
- Language Development
- Cognitive Development
- Perceptual and Motor Development

History–Social Science

This section describes an overview of the alignment of the preschool foundations in History–Social Science with the infant/toddler learning and development foundations and with the California content standards in history–social science for kindergarten. Table 11 shows how the strands and substrands of the preschool learning foundations in History–Social Science align with the infant/toddler foundations and with the kindergarten content standards in history–social science. The detailed alignment between specific preschool learning foundations and specific kindergarten content standards in history–social science may be viewed at http://www. cde.ca.gov/sp/cd/re/documents/ reversealignment.pdf.

As table 11 indicates, the preschool foundations in History–Social Science, particularly the strands **self and society** and **becoming a preschool community member,** are aligned with infant/toddler foundations in the domains of social–emotional development and cognitive development. The preschool substrand *culture and diversity* is aligned with the infant/toddler foundation *identity of self in relation to others.* In preschool, children's sense of self develops and encompasses their cultural, ethnic, and racial identity. The substrand *relationships,* which focuses on children's ability to create and maintain relationships with adults and friends, is aligned with the infant/ toddler foundations *relationships with adults* and *relationships with peers.*

The range of competencies under the strand **becoming a preschool community member (civics),** including *skills for democratic participation,*

responsible conduct, fairness and respect for other people, and *conflict resolution,* are aligned with the following infant/toddler foundations: *interactions with adults, interactions with peers, empathy, impulse control,* and *problem solving.* These social and cognitive competencies set the stage for preschoolers to become responsible and cooperative group members, be attentive to others' feelings and needs, and be capable of negotiation and compromise while resolving conflicts. Finally, the substrands under **sense of place** *navigating familiar locations* and *understanding the physical world through drawings and maps* are aligned with the infant/toddler foundation *spatial relationships,* the early understanding of the location of objects in space.

The kindergarten content standards in history–social science consist of six key standards (K.1–K.6). Table 11 shows the alignment between preschool substrands/foundations and the kindergarten substrands, and table. As table 11 indicates, the first three content standards are aligned with substrands under the strand *self and society.* The substrand *culture and diversity* is aligned with standard K.2, recognition of national and state symbols. The substrand *relationships,* and all substrands under the strand *becoming a preschool community member* (civics), are aligned with kindergarten standard K.1, which focuses on *students' understanding that being a good citizen involves acting in a certain way.* The substrand *social roles and occupations* is directly related to standard K.3, which focuses on children's knowledge of people's occupations at school and in the local community.

The preschool substrand related to sense of time *understanding past events* is aligned with standard K.5, which describes students' ability to put events in temporal order; the substrand *historical changes in people and the world* is aligned with kindergarten standard K.6, the understanding that history relates to events, people, and places. Finally, the preschool substrands related to sense of place *navigating familiar locations* and *understanding the physical world through drawing and maps* are aligned with kindergarten standard K.4, the ability to compare and contrast the locations of people, places, and environments and describe their characteristics.

Table 11

Overview of the Alignment Between the History–Social Science Domain and the California Content Standards

History–Social Science

California Infant/Toddler Learning and Development Foundations	California Preschool Learning Foundations	California Content Standards Kindergarten
Social–Emotional Development **Cognitive Development**	**History–Social Science**	**History–Social Science**
	Self and Society	
Identity of Self in Relation to Others →	Culture and Diversity →	**K.2** Students recognize national and state symbols and icons such as the national and state flags, the bald eagle, and the Statue of Liberty.
Relationships with Adults ⎱ → Relationships with Peers ⎰	Relationships →	**K.1** Students understand that being a good citizen involves acting in certain ways.
	Social Roles and Occupations →	**K.3** Students match simple descriptions of work that people do and the names of related jobs at the school, in the community, and from historical accounts.
	Becoming a Preschool Community Member (Civics)	
Impulse Control ⎱ Interactions with Adults ⎰ → Interactions with Peers Empathy Cause and Effect (Cognitive Development) Problem Solving (Cognitive Development)	⎱ Skills for Democratic Participation ⎰ → Responsible Conduct Fairness and Respect for Other People Conflict Resolution	**K.1** Students understand that being a good citizen involves acting in certain ways.

Table 11 (continued)

History–Social Science

California Infant/Toddler Learning and Development Foundations	California Preschool Learning Foundations	California Content Standards Kindergarten
Social–Emotional Development **Cognitive Development**	**History–Social Science**	**History–Social Science**

Sense of Time (History)

Understanding Past Events → **K.5** Students put events in temporal order using a calendar, placing days, weeks, and months in proper order.

Anticipating and Planning Future Events

Personal History

Historical Changes in People and the World → **K.6** Students understand that history relates to events, people, and places of other times.
K.1 Students understand that being a good citizen involves acting in certain ways.

Sense of Place (Geography and Ecology)

Navigating Familiar Locations
Understanding the Physical World Through Drawings and Maps → **K.4** Students compare and contrast the locations of people, places, and environments and describe their characteristics.

Caring for the Natural World

Spatial Relationships (Cognitive Development) →

Marketplace (Economics)

Exchange

Science

This section describes an overview of the alignment of the preschool foundations in Science with the infant/toddler learning and development foundations and with the California science content standards in kindergarten. Table 12 shows how the strands and substrands of the preschool learning foundations in science align with the infant/toddler foundations and with the kindergarten content standards in science. The detailed alignment between specific preschool learning foundations and specific kindergarten content standards in science may be viewed at http://www.cde.ca.gov/sp/cd/re/documents/reversealignment.pdf.

Core concepts and a range of skills identified in the preschool learning foundations in science emerge and begin to develop during the infant/toddler years. The practice of scientific inquiry draws on children's cognitive, language, social, and physical competencies. Certain cognitive and language abilities are fundamental in the development of scientific concepts and skills. Children's developing abilities to group and sort objects, identify the cause of events and anticipate the effect, engage in a purposeful effort to reach a goal, and explore how something works and how things move and fit in space provide the mental tools for investigating and learning about the characteristics of objects and events in the environment. As table 12 indicates, the infant/toddler foundations in Cognitive Development *classification, cause-and-effect, problem solving,* and *spatial relationships* set the stage for the development of inquiry skills and the learning of concepts in physi-

cal sciences, life sciences, and earth sciences.

Through the process of science, children record observations and communicate ideas and explanations with others. Language and communication skills are fundamental in the development of scientific concepts and skills. Preschool children learn to use language and specific terminology to describe their observations, to plan explorations, and to communicate their findings, explanations, and ideas with others. They also use different forms of communication to record and document information (e.g., oral, written, drawings, photos, graphs, charts). These language and literacy skills emerge at a young age and involve children's ability to understand others, to engage in back-and-forth conversations, and to use expanded vocabulary to express themselves through words. As table 12 indicates, the infant/toddler foundations in *receptive language, expressive language,* and *interest in print* are aligned with the preschool science substrand *documentation and communication.*

The preschool learning foundations in science are also aligned with the kindergarten content standards in science. Table 12 shows the alignment between strands and substrands in the preschool foundations in Science and the corresponding kindergarten strands. As table 12 indicates, the foundations and the kindergarten standards cover the same general categories (strands): **physical sciences, life sciences,** and **earth sciences.** The preschool strand **scientific inquiry** is aligned with the kindergarten strand **investigation and experimentation.** Both the foundations in *observation and investigation* and the kindergarten standards in **investigation and experimentation** focus on children's ability to ask meaningful questions, conduct careful investigations, and observe and describe properties of common objects. The preschool foundations and the kindergarten standards in physical sciences, life sciences, and earth sciences center on the same key ideas: children's ability to observe and describe the properties of materials, the similarities and differences in the appearance and behavior of plants and animals, and the basic characteristics of the earth.

Table 12

Overview of the Alignment Between the Science Domain and the California Content Standards

	Science	
California Infant/Toddler Learning and Development Foundations	California Preschool Learning Foundations	California Content Standards Kindergarten
Cognitive Development **Language Development**	**Science**	**Science**
	Scientific Inquiry	**Investigation and Experimentation**
Problem Solving	Observation and Investigation	Scientific progress is made by asking meaningful questions and conducting careful investigations.
Receptive Language (Language Development) Expressive Language (Language Development) Interest in Print (Language Development)	Documentation and Communication	**Investigation and Experimentation** Scientific progress is made by asking meaningful questions and conducting careful investigations. **Domain: Mathematics** Statistics, Data Analysis, and Probability Students collect information about objects and events in their environment.

Table 12 (continued)

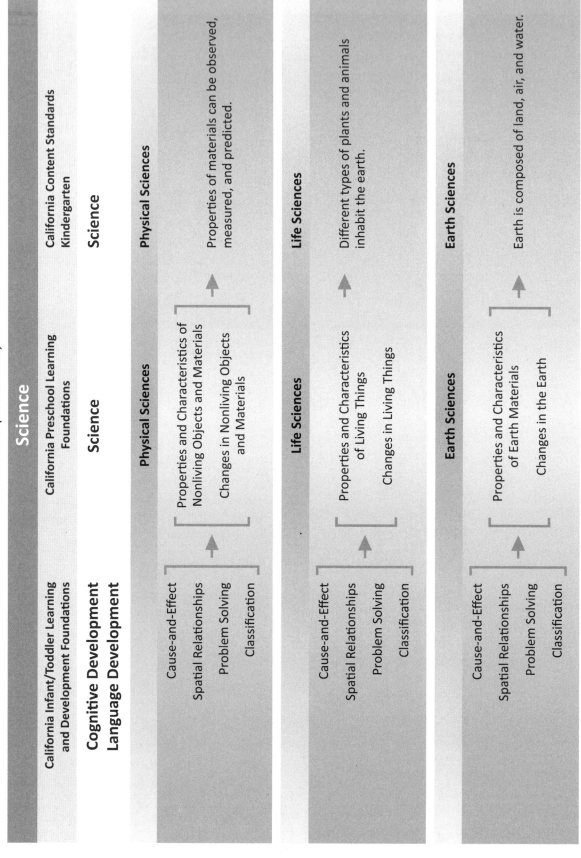

Science

California Infant/Toddler Learning and Development Foundations	California Preschool Learning Foundations	California Content Standards Kindergarten
Cognitive Development **Language Development**	**Science**	**Science**

Physical Sciences

Cause-and-Effect
Spatial Relationships
Problem Solving
Classification
→ Properties and Characteristics of Nonliving Objects and Materials
Changes in Nonliving Objects and Materials
→ Properties of materials can be observed, measured, and predicted.

Life Sciences

Cause-and-Effect
Spatial Relationships
Problem Solving
Classification
→ Properties and Characteristics of Living Things
Changes in Living Things
→ Different types of plants and animals inhabit the earth.

Earth Sciences

Cause-and-Effect
Spatial Relationships
Problem Solving
Classification
→ Properties and Characteristics of Earth Materials
Changes in the Earth
→ Earth is composed of land, air, and water.

An Overview of the Alignment Between the California Preschool Learning Foundations and the Head Start Child Development and Early Learning Framework

This section provides a summary of the alignment between the *California Preschool Learning Foundations* and the *Head Start Learning Framework*. The detailed alignment, which delineates the alignment between specific preschool learning foundations and specific components in the *Head Start Learning Framework* for each domain, may be viewed at http://www.cde.ca.gov/sp/cd/re/documents/reversealignment.pdf.

The Head Start Act (as amended in 2007) promotes alignment of the *Head Start Learning Framework*) with state curriculum, assessment, and standards. In California, these standards are represented by the *California Preschool Learning Foundations, Volumes 1–3* (CDE 2008, 2010, and forthcoming).

The California Head Start Collaboration Office—in partnership with the California Head Start Association, California Center of the Office of Head Start Training and Technical Assistance Network, California Department of Education, and WestEd—spearheaded the development of an alignment of the *Head Start Learning Framework with the California Preschool Learning Foundations* to address the needs of Head Start programs.

This document supports Head Start education managers and education supervisors by showing how these two sources align with each other and the similarities of goals for children in all areas of learning and development. The alignment of the *Head Start Learn-*

ing Framework with the *California Preschool Learning Foundations* provides a valuable resource to make sure all the components of education in an early childhood program—curriculum goals, teaching strategies, and assessment—are coordinated and aligned.

The California Center of the Office of Head Start Training and Technical Assistance Network can provide support to programs through the process of reviewing the alignment of the *Head Start Learning Framework* and the *California Preschool Learning Foundations* to ensure the programs' curriculum, assessment, and school-readiness goals are also aligned with these two documents.

The *California Preschool Learning Foundations* and the *Head Start Learning Framework* share common goals—to strengthen preschool education and young children's readiness for school and to promote all aspects of child learning and development in early childhood programs. The California preschool learning foundations describe knowledge and skills that most children, with appropriate support, can be expected to exhibit as they complete their first and second year of preschool. Foundations are established for children at around 48 months of age and at around 60 months of age. Nine domains of learning and development are addressed: Social–Emotional Development, Language and Literacy, English-Language Development, Mathematics, Visual and Performing Arts, Physical Development, Health, History–Social Science, and Science. The *Head Start Learning Framework* delineates the developmental building blocks essential for children's school and long-term success. The Framework is intended for children three to five years old and is organized into 11 domains: Physical Development & Health, Social & Emotional Development, Approaches to Learning, Logic & Reasoning, Language Development, English Language Development, Literacy Knowledge & Skills, Mathematics Knowledge & Skills, Science Knowledge & Skills, Creative Arts Expression, and Social Studies Knowledge & Skills.

About the Alignment

The following analysis describes the alignment between the *California Preschool Learning Foundations* and the *Head Start Learning Framework.* The alignment shows the **ways in which these two sources correspond in content and share similar goals for children in all areas of learning and development.** In this alignment, the nine domains of the preschool foundations are presented in the same order and structure shown as the original *California Preschool Learning Foundations* volumes. For each foundation, the alignment indicates the components in the *Head Start Learning Framework* that correspond in content. In other words, the preschool foundations are the starting point of the alignment, and components from the 11 domains in the Framework are aligned with the preschool learning foundations.

An alternative version of the alignment, one in which components of the preschool learning foundations are aligned with the *Head Start Learning Framework,* may be viewed at http:// www.cde.ca.gov/sp/cd/re/documents/reversealignment.pdf . The 11 domains in the *Head Start Learning Framework* are presented in the same structure and order as the original Framework. For each domain in the

Framework, the alignment indicates the components of the preschool foundations that correspond in content.

While the *Head Start Learning Framework* generally applies to children who are three to five years old, the preschool learning foundations are separated at two age levels, showing a progression on a continuum of learning. Foundations are established for children at around 48 months of age (four years) and at around 60 months of age (five years). The alignment of the preschool learning foundations and the Framework presents only the foundations for children at around 48 months of age, a midpoint in the age range addressed in the *Head Start Learning Framework.* The complete set of foundations, including the foundations for children at about 60 months of age, can be found in the *California Preschool Learning Foundations, Volumes 1–3* (CDE 2008, 2010, and forthcoming).

General Alignment at the Domain Level

Table 13 outlines the nine domains in the preschool learning foundations and the corresponding domain(s) in the *Head Start Learning Framework.* The table also delineates other domains in the Framework with content corresponding to the foundations. For example, the Social–Emotional Development domain of the preschool foundations is aligned with the **Social & Emotional Development** domain in the Framework, as well as with components from two additional domains in the Framework: namely, **Approaches to Learning and Logic & Reasoning.** Table 13 shows how both the *California Preschool Learning Foundations* and the *Head Start Learning Frame-*

Table 13

Overview Alignment of the Domains in the California Preschool Learning Foundations and the Head Start Child Development and Early Learning Framework

Domains in the California Preschool Learning Foundations	Domains in the Head Start Child Development and Early Learning Framework	Additional Domains in the Head Start Framework with Corresponding Content
Social–Emotional Development	Social & Emotional Development	Approaches to Learning Logic & Reasoning
Language and Literacy	Language Development Literacy Knowledge & Skills	
English-Language Development	English Language Development	Literacy Knowledge & Skills
Mathematics	Mathematics Knowledge & Skills	Logic & Reasoning Approaches to Learning
Visual and Performing Arts	Creative Arts Expression	Logic & Reasoning
Physical Development	Physical Development & Health	
Health	Physical Development & Health	
History–Social Science	Social Studies Knowledge & Skills	Social & Emotional Development
Science	Science Knowledge & Skills	Approaches to Learning Logic & Reasoning

work cover parallel content, though some of it is organized differently.

As evident in table 13, each domain in the preschool learning foundations maps to a major corresponding domain in the *Head Start Learning Framework*. For example, the Mathematics domain in the preschool foundations is aligned with the Mathematics Knowledge & Skills domain from the Framework. In addition, some of the domains align with multiple domains from the Framework. The Mathematics domain, for example, is also aligned with components from the Approaches to Learning and Logic & Reasoning domains. The Language and Literacy domain has two corresponding domains in the *Head Start Learning Framework*:

(1) Language Development and (2) Literacy Knowledge & Skills. The preschool foundations in **English-Language Development** are aligned with the Head Start **English Language Development** domain and with components in the Head Start **Literacy Knowledge & Skills** domain. Also, the preschool foundations in History–Social Science are aligned with components in the Head Start domains of **Social Studies Knowledge & Skills** and **Social & Emotional Development.** Although the **Approaches to Learning** and **Logic & Reasoning** domains appear only in the *Head Start Learning Framework*, the content of those two domains is covered by different domains of the preschool learning

foundations: Mathematics, Social–Emotional Development, Visual and Performing Arts, and Science.

Alignment within Each Domain

The extent of the alignment between the *California Preschool Learning Foundations* and the *Head Start Learning Framework* becomes clear when the elements within each domain of these two resources are directly lined up next to each other. In the preschool learning foundations, each domain consists of several main strands, and each strand consists of substrands. The foundations are organized under the substrands. In the Head Start Learning Framework, each domain includes elements and examples to illustrate key knowledge, behaviors, or skills within the element. The alignment draws connections between (1) the strands and substrands within each domain of the preschool foundations and the corresponding Head Start domain elements; and (2) the foundations under each substrand and the corresponding examples in the Head Start Learning Framework. Table 14 shows how different components in each document align with or match each other.

In sum, for each of the nine domains in the preschool foundations, the alignment draws the connection between the strands and substrands in the preschool learning foundations domain and the corresponding domain elements in the *Head Start Learning Framework*, and between specific foundations in each substrand and the corresponding examples in the Framework.

Analysis of the Alignment

The alignment indicates a close correspondence between the domains and foundations in the preschool learning foundations and the matching components in the *Head Start Learning Framework*. Overall, as evident in the tables, for almost every substrand in the preschool learning foundations, there is at least one domain element in the Framework that reflects the content of the corresponding preschool foundations. The few substrands in the preschool foundations with no corresponding content in the *Head Start Learning Framework* are *social conventions* in the English-Language Development domain, *body awareness* in the Physical Development domain, *self-regulation of eating* in the Health

Table 14

Organization of the California Preschool Learning Foundations and the Head Start Child Development and Early Learning Framework

California Preschool Learning Foundations	Head Start Child Development and Early Learning Framework
Domain	Domain
Strands	---------
Substrands	Domain elements
Foundations	Examples

domain, and *marketplace (economics)* in the History–Social Science domain. Similarly, a close inspection of the Head Start alignment indicates that 36 of the 37 domain elements in the *Head Start Learning Framework* have a corresponding substrand with similar content in the preschool foundations.

The only domain element with no direct correspondence in the preschool foundations is *physical health status* (Head Start, Physical Development & Health). This domain element addresses the health aspects that programs need to monitor in order to ensure children's physical well-being. Although *physical health status* is not addressed in the alignment, this domain element is significant, and programs should follow local policy for monitoring children's physical health status.

In some domains, there is a noteworthy amount of direct correspondence, both in content and in level of specificity, between the preschool foundations and the corresponding examples in the *Head Start Learning Framework.* This correspondence is particularly evident in domains such as Social–Emotional Development, Language and Literacy, and Mathematics. In domains such as English- Language Development, Visual and Performing Arts, Physical Development, History–Social Science, and Science, the preschool foundations are more detailed. Even so, the preschool foundations and the Framework cover the same key content areas in those domains.

Bibliography

California Department of Education. *California Infant/Toddler Learning & Development Foundations.* Sacramento: California Department of Education, 2009.

———. *California Preschool Learning Foundations (Volume 1).* Sacramento: California Department of Education, 2008.

———. *California Preschool Learning Foundations (Volume 2).* Sacramento: California Department of Education, 2010.

———. *California Preschool Learning Foundations (Volume 3).* Sacramento: California Department of Education, forthcoming.

———. *English–Language Arts Content Standards for California Public Schools, Kindergarten Through Grade Twelve.* Sacramento: California Department of Education, 1998.

———. *Health Education Content Standards for California Public Schools, Kindergarten Through Grade Twelve.* Sacramento: California Department of Education, 2009.

———. *History–Social Science Content Standards for California Public Schools, Kindergarten Through Grade Twelve.* Sacramento: California Department of Education, 2000.

———. *Mathematics Content Standards for California Public Schools, Kindergarten Through Grade Twelve.* Sacramento: California Department of Education, 1999.

———. *Physical Education Model Content Standards for California Public Schools, Kindergarten Through Grade Twelve.* Sacramento: California Department of Education, 2006.

———. *Science Content Standards for California Public Schools, Kindergarten Through Grade Twelve.* Sacramento: California Department of Education, 2000.

———. *Visual and Performing Arts Content Standards for California Public Schools, Kindergarten Through Grade Twelve.* Sacramento: California Department of Education, 2001.

Sacramento County Office of Education. *California's Common Core Content Standards for English Language Arts & Literacy in History Social Studies, Science, and Technical Subjects.* Sacramento, 2010. http://www.scoe.net/castandards/agenda/2010/ela_ccs_recommendations.pdf [Outside Source] (accessed April 4, 2012).

———. *California's Common Core Content Standards for Mathematics.* Sacramento, 2010. http://www.scoe.net/castandards/agenda/2010/math_ccs_recomendations.pdf [Outside Source] (accessed April 4, 2012).

U.S. Department of Health and Human Services, Administration for Children and Families, Office of Head Start. *The Head Start Child Development and Learning Framework: Promoting Positive Outcomes in Early Childhood Programs Serving Children 3–5 Years Old.* Arlington, VA: U.S. Department of Health and Human Services: Administration for Children and Families, Office of Head Start, 2010.